What is your request?
Even if it be half the kingdom
You may have it.

— The Scroll of Esther (5:3)

HALF
THE
KINGDOM

Seven Jewish Feminists

EDITED BY FRANCINE ZUCKERMAN

Véhicule Press

Published with the assistance of The Canada Council.

Cover design: J.W. Stewart
Typesetting and design: Paul Davies, ECW Type & Art
Printing: Imprimerie d'Édition Marquis Ltée
Photographs on the following pages courtesy of Barry Perles and the
National Film Board of Canada: 14, 30, 56, 70, 106, 146.
Photograph on page 155 by Ian Clifford.

Canadian Cataloguing In Publication Data

Main entry under title:
    Half the kingdom : seven Jewish feminists

Includes bibliographical references.
ISBN 1-55065-003-3

    1. Women, Jewish. 2. Feminism. 3. Women in Judaism.
I. Zuckerman, Francine

HQ1172.H35 1992   305.48'696   C92-090701-6

Distributed in Canada by General Publishing, 30 Lesmill Road,
Don Mills, Ontario M3B 2T6, and in the United States by Inland
Book Company (East Haven, CT).

Véhicule Press, P.O.B. 125, Place du Parc Station, Montreal,
Quebec, Canada H2W 2M9

Printed in Canada on acid-free paper.

CONTENTS

This book is dedicated to my beloved parents Annita and Jack Zuckerman (my mother gave me the drive, my father gave me the dreams), and to my dear friends who continue to encourage my strength and renew my spirit: Debra Plotkin, Helen Zukerman, Honey Dresher, Norma Joseph, Liliana Kleiner and Keyawis; and to my nephews Noah Seth and Jordan Alexander who will be the next generation of enlightened, courageous, feminist men.

i found God in myself
& i loved her
i loved her fiercely

     — Ntozeki Shange
     (from *Coloured Girls Who Have Considered*
     Suicide, When Rainbow is Enuf)

PREFACE

Although *Half the Kingdom*, the film, began in 1983, it was conceived many years earlier. The film was inspired by the struggle of many women who continue to seek their own way to integrate feminism with their Jewish roots.

As a feminist Jew I have experienced many contradictions: the pain of alienation, the pleasure of community, the joy of the Jewish spirit. We have all chosen diverse paths. Mine moves away from any element of tradition to find a new creation. This new conception upholds the Jewish spirit, yet diverts radically from religion as we know it. In my need to find new ways, this process has sent me on a journey of which *Half the Kingdom* is only part.

I grew up in Regina, Saskatchewan, then a small Canadian prairie town, where there was only an Orthodox synagogue. I attended with my family and sat separately from my father, separate from the men as tradition dictates. From a child's egocentric point of view, it did not feel right — the men had access to everything. Early on I was left with a sense of injustice.

When I graduated from film school I thought that I was ready to make a film. I soon realized that I had skills to learn and a craft to perfect. After several years of working on other people's films it became apparent that it was important for me to embark on a film project that would attempt to explain what it meant to be a Jewish woman in the last decade of the twentieth century. *Half the Kingdom* was to be the most difficult undertaking I had ever attempted.

So I began . . . not quite knowing where to begin or how to begin. What did I want to say? How was it to be financed? What began as a personal journey, based on years of my own questions, became a half-million dollar National Film Board co-production with a crew of over twenty people that took six years to complete. My journey became the communal journeys of many women — the subjects of the film, the co-director, co-producers, consultants, the writer — the whole team. The process had a profound effect on many of us.

For months I travelled across Canada, the United States, and Israel. I had many questions. Hours were spent in homes, offices, and cafés with women who were also searching.

Each one of the women in the film affected my life in a different way. Naomi Goldenberg was with me from the beginning — searching, probing, and guiding. She too was on a journey — looking for her place as a Jew. Elyse Goldstein made a major impact on me and the Canadian Jewish community. Alice Shalvi linked me to a network; my lifeline to the Israeli women's community. She gave me strength in her strength and energy. Michele Landsberg was an inspiration to me even before I met her. She was always on the cutting edge, dealing with what I thought were the key feminist issues. Shulamit Aloni was at the forefront of the Israeli political scene. Her determination, her unrelenting commitment, and her incredible vigour greatly stimulated my work. When I first met Norma Joseph I knew she had a place in this film. Her sincerity and determination gave me great courage. She became my guiding light and I depended on her throughout the process. I called Esther Broner one Friday evening when I was in New York City. Without further ado, she invited me to her Friday night feast. Around the table sat a diverse group of fascinating people. I watched Esther and I listened to her. It did not take me long to realize that the woman whose writings I had come to admire, would be as provocative in the film as she was in her books. Many women had an impact on the film who could not appear in it. Women like Marcia Falk, Judith Plaskow, Paula Hyman, Blu Greenberg, Carol Rose,

Savina Teubel, Zippoah Greenfield, Frida Forman, Susan Weidman Schneider, Rachel Adler, and Jane Litman. I thank them for their silent but significant contribution.

We had to make difficult choices. Only seven women could be in this onehour film. During this process I worked closely with coexecutive producer Heather Marshall and codirector/editor Roushell Goldstein. We became a team, making decisions and choices together. Our writer Elaine Goldstein assisted with fundraising and was a great asset. Liz Magnes was drafted from Jerusalem to compose the music. Kathy Avrich Johnson was a great advisor and legal counsel.

Heather Marshall and I pounded the pavement to raise the necessary funds. On the advice of Dorothy Reitman we tried innovative grassroots fundraising to gather Jewish women together to fund a film about Jewish women. Although the events almost cost as much as we raised we learned a great deal about community fundraising. Finally we collected enough money for a oneday shoot.

The day we brought Naomi Goldenberg, Elyse Goldstein, and Norma Joseph together for what seemed to be an endless shooting day, I realized we were on our way. We produced a twelve minute clip that convinced Beverly Shaffer of the National Film Board's Studio D to join the team and Rina Fraticelli, Executive Producer of Studio D to support the film. We landed a presale with TV Ontario, and funding from Telefilm Canada and the Zukerman Charitable Foundation was secured. (Helen Zukerman was the major private contributor to the film). The money was in place and we were ready to shoot. After four years my dream was about to come true.

After several very long weeks of shooting the film, the editing process began. Roushel Goldstein put together a succinct, fluid, and provocative sequence of events in four months of cutting, re-cutting, test screenings, and editing room debates. The narration and music were added and *Half the Kingdom* became a reality.

The Montreal screening was a very special time for me and my family. The response was tremendous. I toured with the film as it premiered across Canada and the United States. I went with the film to the International Film Festival in London, the Films de Femmes in France, the cinémathèques in Israel, and the Jewish Film Festival in San Francisco and Berkeley. *Half the Kingdom* sparked intense discussion. Some men were offended by the film, perturbed because they were not represented. Women hugged me and thanked me for making the film. One woman was so inspired by Elyse Goldstein that she decided to return to her studies to become an Anglican minister. I encountered opposition to the issues from the Israeli audience, quiet interest from the British audience, subtle anti-Semitism from the French audience, and estrangement from a radical segment of the San Francisco audience.

When the tour was extended to include many small Jewish communities across Canada the response to the film was often intense and very emotional. In one city, a man who had opposed showing the film in his community, told me that I had converted him. The film had reminded him of his mother who had recently passed away. He introduced me with tears in his eyes, speaking of his mother and her contribution as a feminist.

When Simon Dardick, publisher at Véhicule Press, approached me with the idea of a book based on the film, I realized it was an opportunity to extend our audience. This book is based on inter-views from the film and therefore will reflect a speaking, rather than written quality. Editing the transcripts, I again became excited about the issues that were raised by the seven women participants in over fifteen hours of film footage. There are many more books to be written, and films to be made, on the relationship of women with Judaism. I hope that *Half the Kingdom*, the film and the book, will inspire more thought and inquiry, more rebellion and reform.

Heather Marshall (executive producer), Francine Zuckerman (producer/ director/executive producer), Norma Joseph (participant and consultant), Roushell Goldstein (director/editor) at the Gemini Awards, Toronto, 1990.

❧ *E.M. Broner is a novelist, playwright, and Jewish feminist ritualist living in New York City. She has published five books including* Her Mothers *(Indiana University Press, 1975) and* A Weave of Women *(Indiana University, 1978). She is the recipient of two National Endowment for the Arts Awards and is Professor Emeritus at Wayne State University, Detroit. Her new work,* The Telling, *based on the annual feminist seder in New York City will be published by Harper, San Francisco in 1993. She is currently involved in a work-in-progress entitled* The Repair Shop.

ESTHER BRONER

My nice dad died — he was a journalist and a Jewish scholar. The melody he played on his typewriter was a melody I could sing and I knew I could be a writer. When his song was finished it was unbearable for me not to mourn him properly. He wanted a *kaddish*, a daily prayer.

I have two brothers, but I, as the eldest, did not want to give that over to them. It was a responsibility and a duty and I wanted to be able to do enough. I wanted it to suffice. It's not common for a woman to say *kaddish* because you put yourself in a male *minyan* and a woman is not counted in that *minyan* of ten men. You know that you will go where you will never be counted. You know you will stand behind a *mehitzah*, a curtain, in a separate part of the *shul*. In some synagogues you stand in a balcony, and you are not ever acknowledged as being part of the group. You have to do that rigorously for eleven months.

I didn't think about any of this at the time. I was so inconsolable that I thought here was a way to spend every morning talking to my dad and at the end of that time maybe our conversation would be finished and I could go on to other business. I didn't know that the curtain would be such an important part of the room or of my psyche.

When I chose a *shul* to recite *kaddish* for my father I chose in innocence and I chose convenience. Since I always went to the neighbourhood school and neighbourhood swimming pool, I thought the neighbourhood *shul* would be just as good.

My first day at the *shul* I met a gaunt, grey-haired woman. When I sat down she said, "Not there, not there. We're not allowed over there. Come here behind the *shmatah*, the rag." And then she said, "Those bastards, it's never thick enough for them. I don't know whether they're standing up or sitting down. I don't know whether the Torah is open or closed. I don't know whether it's summer or winter. But this is my last day here and may they all burn in hell!" I saw her leave wide-eyed and did not know that within a short time I would be talking just like that woman.

That was my introduction to the *shul*. Actually, though, it housed my grief for eleven months, which was the required period of mourning. My dear dad was supposed to plead his case on the twelfth month and since he is a writer I know he pleaded it very well.

The rabbi usually managed to gather a *minyan*. Sometimes we would have to wait for an hour for the required ten men to arrive. I, on the other hand, was always called half-a-man. They would say, "Here comes half-a-man," when I came into the room.

I would refuse to stand behind the *mehitzah*. It was an oppression, an indignity, and I began to feel like I was wearing a *chador*, that I was in *purdah* or that I had taken a nun's veil. During that winter I went to Macy's and bought gaudier and gaudier clothes — phos-phorescent orange raincoats, luminous purple and green jackets. I began to understand why Orthodox women dress so well; it is to fight their invisibility.

In the *shul* two things were happening at the same time: the rabbi's longing for *shalom bayit*, peace in the household, and the rage of the men because I was invading their territory. Every day in the morning prayer service they read the story of the *akedah*, the binding of Isaac, of Abraham with a knife, the threatening knife above Isaac. It gradually became clear to me why the men in the *shul* declared themselves 'masters of death.' The men thought, in a sense, that God was holding that knife over them and that life was very close to death and at any time could be taken. I, on the other hand, was life-pro-ducing, which they could never be. Their reaction went from disapproval to terrible rage, to violence. One fanatic once tried to strangle me with the *mehitzah* when I would not stand behind the curtain. He called me *zona*, whore! I began to understand the connection between sexuality and religiosity — a terrible, terrible hatred of women.

The men spent a great deal of energy trying to make the *mehitzah* more and more opaque. At first the separation was on a clothes-rack and someone bumped his ankle against it and said, "This is liable to kill somebody and they'll sue us." It was a rack they wheeled back and forth to hide me and I always very stubbornly pushed it away. Then they hung a cheap, gold-coloured lacy curtain and again I would stand outside of it and this was unsatisfying to them. The very religious felt they could not *doven* (pray) seeing the face of a woman.

One time I came into the *shul* and the new, fourth *mehitzah* was a shower curtain. I used to swim across the street at the Y. When I saw the shower curtains, I reached into my gym bag past the soap and the towel, pulled out my bathing cap and put it on my head and then opened the curtains and *dovened*. The shower curtains did not last too long and the next set of curtains turned out to be the Great Wall of China from floor to ceiling.

I said to the men, "Think how much time, energy, even expense has been expended against one woman and thereby all women." The *mehitzah* forced me to be seated on one side of the room in a limited, confined space, while the rest of the group had the ninety-nine percent of the room on the other side.

The bench I was sitting on was the woman's bench, a small space maybe big enough for three women. It was always piled with the men's winter clothes, and sometimes with the charity box. I would clear it all off but it was as if there was room on that bench for everything else but a woman.

After about six weeks of this interesting experience, I sent out an S.O.S. I'm part of a group. We call ourselves the Seder Sisters and we have been doing a women's *seder* for about thirteen years, ever since I first wrote *The Stolen Legacy: A Woman's Haggadah* with Naomi Nimrod in Haifa. I said, "Dear *minyan* mates, I have been here this long. There has been some accommodation. I understand something about the men of the *shul*. They are beginning to under-stand something about my needs but I have such a longing to extend beyond myself, not to be just a small shadow here. Please come to me so that I can have a *minyan* of women."

They showed up that Sunday. I think it was March 29th. There were about thirteen or fourteen of them who had dismissed their patients, left their embassies, their art, their writing, their families. These wonderful professional women came from everywhere in the city and from Brooklyn. The men were startled. At first they said to each other worriedly, "There are more of them than there are of us. Soon they'll take over."

18

I had provided for a *kiddish* following the service which included, what they rarely had, a sheet of expensive lox. Such a look came over their faces. They said, "Remember what it was like in the old days when the *shul* was Conservative and we had such a nice *kiddish*."

Things eased up a bit and that *minyan* of women gave me courage, but this was only six weeks in and I had to get through the rest of the year myself. In that whole time I seldom saw another woman, yet the wrath still poured upon me on occasion.

The *shul* was a house of lonely, elderly men. The day stretched emptily before them. Sometimes it was my visiting them for a moment, a bit of softness that was their only connection with the world of family. They begged me to stay after the service and have a little *kiddish* with them, a little wine. I sometimes did or I would refuse saying, "We pray separately, we eat separately." The men would ask me what I was doing during the day. Some of them were reluctant to let me go. Most of them did not work, or the retirees among them would occasionally visit their old place of business and hoped to be made welcome.

The rabbi had the difficult job of organizing the *minyan* and getting his regular congregants to keep coming and, also, to keep me from being totally humiliated and discouraged. It was a fine line. Because he was Orthodox, the rabbi believed in the *mehitzah*. It pained him that I fought so rebelliously. Once he said to my husband, "Can't she just forget this and understand that it's just a matter between her and her father? Can't she put principle aside?" Bob responded, "But Esther can't put principle aside."

I wrote a memoir about that instructive year and called it "Mornings and Mourning: A Kaddish Journal." The magazine, *Tikkun*, published a large section of it.

19

There are few rituals for any women in any religion that are positive, inclusive. We have had to invent our own.

I went to a gathering of Roman Catholic women, a group called Woman Church. There the women were kneading bread together, the shewbread, and regenderizing prayer. When we said Grace, the women at Woman Church used the Hebrew word, *rouach*, spirit, wind, as an inclusive for God. Elsewhere, at another Catholic women's conference, I heard God addressed as, Mother, Sister, Lover.

These are astounding changes in the most fundamentalist of churches. If that is happening; if Roman Catholic women have such a longing for inclusion, a longing that is spear-headed by nuns, then Jewish women, who by and large are from a more liberal tradition, should surely rise in wrath and write there own rituals. This is actually happening in plenitude — women's liturgical songs, ceremonies, more holiday tapes and albums that I can keep up with. All dealing with new ritual.

'Ritual' is such an interesting word. It means 'rite' as in rites of passage; it means "arithmetic, rhythm" — all that which is orderly, repetitive and which honours our lives.

There was nothing that marked women. There was no parade to mark the daily heroic. There are changes we see: noticing that your daughter has started to bleed and that her life is forever different. Nothing happens to honour that at home or in the house of worship. It is noticing, at the other end, when you have stopped bleeding (a *schlep* that goes on for about ten years), and nobody comes by and touches you and says "I name you crone."

Nor is it noticing the terrible things that happen to women: the abuse, violence in the family, the AIDS epidemic affecting so many young women, breast cancer that takes one in four women. We must be politically active and ceremonially observant of these events, to heal them as much as we can.

In 1984, when the University of Southern California and the University of Judaism had a conference called "The Shekina: Illuminating the Unwritten Scroll," they asked me to do a ritual at the end of it. As any anthropologist knows, rituals require song and artifact. I thought about that a long time and decided we needed a scroll that had things written on it that you did not find in your usual Jewish scrolls. Anthropologist Gelya Frank and I sat up all night working attaching wooden dowels to butcher block paper. We created blank scrolls, wrapped them in velvet and tied them with golden twine.

When the women entered the room, Evie Rosenbloom, a wonderful cantor, sang "Nigun of the Shekina." The women saw the scrolls in their velvet casings leaning against a cabinet, they knew they were going to have a spiritual experience. The cantor and I unwrapped the scrolls and I said, "You will make these holy by writing down the sayings of your mothers, of your women mentors or your teachers, your grandmothers, your lovers, the women of importance in your life." As the women knelt to write, I could see the paper puckered under their tears. These were women and men who had never realized that what their bubbies told them, what their mamma told them, what Virginia Woolf told them, what Emma Goldman told them, were holy words!

After we dressed the scrolls we began dancing with them. The scrolls were placed on chairs and lifted like brides. Later, Professor Frank had the scrolls transcribed and put into a special casing. This event gave permission for women to create rituals, to declare holidays, to declare the words of their matrilineage sacred.

Savina Teubel, an author invented another holiday, *Simchat*

Chochama, Holiday of Wisdom. Savina was turning sixty. She came dressed in a white *kittle*, and songs were composed for her by Cantor Debbie Friedman and new lyrics were also written by the poet Marcia Falk for other songs.

Savina was making exodus from one period in her life to another, crossing borders, so she adapted "Genesis," God's words to Abraham, "Go forth," as her paradigm. Only Savina regenderized it, so that it was as if Sarah were to hear God's command, "You, woman, go forth, to a land you do not know and you shall be a blessing."

Every time we do these ceremonies, the tears abound, and, each time, it is as if we were in a new land and had to find our own path. There is no cartography that has preceded us. Each ceremony that we do is done for the first time. We are snow angels in the snow.

We did a Farewell to the Uterus ceremony — we being my network, the Seder Sisters. One of us had a hysterectomy, and it was in the spring, during the time of new fruits, Shavuoth. The woman was dressed in white like a bride and declared a crone, set in the centre of the circle of women and fed these new fruits, as she had fed those inside of her, those outside of her.

We then, this *minyan* of women, talked about what it was to have a uterus and not have used it, or to have aborted it. We talked of being women with and without uteruses. We worried that, without a uterus, we would be less feminine, then we reminded ourselves of what feminine had meant when we were young — the discomfort of it — the pointy, boned bras, the big curlers that gave your neck a crick when you slept, the rubber girdles. All of that self-conscious ness just to be "feminine." And we laughed and looked at one another and we looked as good as any people on this earth, as feminine as we may have wanted or rejected. We declared, instead of an old and trite myth of femininity, a new myth — "an external

22

uterus with which we could nurture those in need, the world."

This experience was a comfort to us all.

On books and writing

When I was writing *Her Mothers* in the mid-seventies, women were not searching. I thought, why should the *Odyssey* be the paradigm? Why should Odysseus be the searcher of literature? Wasn't his wife Penelope in her own search? So I thought of my book as a 'Penelopiad,' a search of a mother for a daughter, a daughter for the mother and ultimately the search for herself that was *Her Mothers*. It was a search that took her everywhere, especially into herself. It was a hard book to write. I had no models for that kind of book, a *künstlerroman*, a book about an artist searching for herself. Once the mother and daughter had found each other, it seemed to me a new kind of negotiation, a peace had been reached, a new lineage. From that tangled, loving, and painful relationship between mother and daughter came another kind of book, something more supportive, joyous, ritualistic; a new way for women to meet, to come together. That is when I wrote *A Weave of Women*.

On a 3x5 card I penned instructions to myself: "I want to make a new calendar for women and write it in an elegiac prose." I wrote about a group of women living in a little stone house in Jerusalem who returned dignity to each other, exorcised the demons, and helped to raise one another. People still ask me for the address of that 'stone house.'

I had "solved," in literary fashion, the problem of the relationship of mother to daughter, of women to one another; then the earth pressed heavily against me, the world and its news. It seemed to me we were living in an apocalyptic time. I am active politically. That

23

is the way I live — active rather than passive — trying to change the tenor of things. In my books I solve what I can't solve in my life.

In my work-in-progress, "The Repair Shop," I have a mystical figure who becomes political. You first see this figure, dressed in a caftan, a long black traditional coat, wearing a *yarmulke* (skull cap). This is an Orthodox person.

Gradually you discover that this person is a woman rabbi. She guards the Sabbath and hence walks miles every day to and from her place of chaplaincy. She walks to the downtown hospital where she is chaplain and she walks home on the Sabbath to the Upper West Side. On the way she encounters the people who will become part of her congregation. With them she will open up a shop, a spiritual shop, which she will call 'The Repair Shop,' *tikun olam*, from the Jewish concept that we are here on this earth to repair. Her congregation consists of people in wheelchairs, people on park benches, patients in the hospital, lovers who lost their loves, and mothers who lost their sons. In these encounters, the rabbi finds her own power. She and her congregation heal themselves and one another. In so doing, they begin the process of creating a new world.

Family

I have two families. I have my family, my marital, biological family, and I have my family of friends. My biological family is my past, context, safety net, and future. My family of friends is the family that gives me permission, that alters my shape. It makes me more mature and it makes me more myself. I have individual friends and communal friends. For instance, we writers at P.E.N. America formed a P.E.N. Women's Committee when we realized how denigrated women were in this important organization. We determined that the work of women would be our matter of concern. We resuscitate the work of writers that is deserving but which has been neglected. We hold programmes to explicate, to honour these works. We honour our foremothers and, therefore, honour ourselves. We are a professional Old Girls' Network by hearing each other, critiquing the work of one another, introducing each other to our contacts and caring about each other. In this way people like Mary Gordon, Grace Paley, Marilyn French, and Vivian Gornick, form a community. Some are older, some are younger, and in some ways, they are my mothers, and in some ways, my daughters. That to me is a community of women: helpful, loving, and professionally there for you.

There is also my Seder Sisters community, which is where I go when I am in deep spiritual trouble.

How do I reconcile all of this with home? I have two homes: my home of family that is my context, my reference, my extension, and then I have my community. Often I bring one community to the other. Ideally we should have both kinds of families.

Risk-taking

I am concerned about the fear women have of taking risks. We are very concerned about our safety, and for good reason. We have been occupied for a long time. We are patrilocal — we go where our husbands take us, where their work is. We are shaped by their needs; we take their names and speak in their voices. We lock our doors; we lock our hearts and sometimes we lock our bodies and our minds. What I am hoping do is to help women take risks by creating ceremony and community.

At an international conference, "The Empowerment of Jewish Women" held in Jerusalem in December 1988, I had hoped by word, by metaphor, to encourage women to risk peace during this time of the Intifada.

Once, a while ago, when I lived and taught in Jerusalem, I noticed a loose piece of dirty plastic on the street. It was a yellow warning in Hebrew, Arabic, and English: "Caution. Danger. Underground electrical cables." I picked it up and saved it as an artifact. I was interested that the entire population was being warned that something subterranean, something very dangerous could happen to all of its citizens. I was interested that there were potholes, electrical shorts, the possibility of an explosion. The finding of this artifact preceded the Intifada.

When I spoke at this conference in a meeting open to the entire public, I wanted to shock, to surprise, to put on the yellow plastic strip as a *tallis*, a prayer shawl, and I wanted to pray for peace — to recognize the dangers underfoot, to reach out and ask for peace. I called upon a divinity student to blow the *shofar*, the ram's horn, and said that this is sounded at the time of New Moon, holiday, and war. And I said let it be the sound that resonates for peace.

I would like to approach my opposite, my other, the Palestinian woman and say, "Let's extend our hands to one another. Let's extend our voices. Let us look at the size of the other, into the eyes of the other, and we will recognize ourselves. Somewhere it must be possible to find a common tongue, a common border."

That is what I hoped the ceremony would do. Change the world. *Tikkun Olam* — heal the world.

ESTHER BRONER
℔ *Excerpt from her work-in-progress, "The Repair Shop."*

Where the little Rabbi's feet trod dusk follows. This is Friday at the Farmer's Market in Union Square. It seems to the Rabbi that a storm is brewing for the wind whistles, hisses, whimpers. The Rabbi's neck hurts from turning abruptly to look behind her. A portly cyclist tries to hide near the equestrian statue of George Washington. Slender Lafayette, ascetic Gandhi, both statues, do not provide enough cover for his cycle and his stomach. Another man passes the cyclist in haste pursuing the little Rabbi. This man is covered from head to foot with no part of him exposed. He is dressed like a desert dweller. He slips on autumn leaves. Behind him are the skid marks from the juice of maple and oak. The little Rabbi feels a sudden chill and clutches her caftan closer about her.

No one else feels that early, wintry blast for the customers in the park are walking bushes. They carry branches of red leaves, of golden leaves with crimson berries, of freshly-cut daisies and potted palms. If they stood still the park attendants would water them. The clouds above are feather and scale. They beat like great wings. It is a special time. *Tsimtsum*, the moment before creation when God takes a deep breath and creates a vacuum and within that vacuum both evil and good thrive. At such a time Satan hisses into one ear and the angel blows softly into the other. At such a time God and human can see backward, can pierce darkness, and distance. The market is closing. The Rabbi must rise, also, for the long trek home, but winds tuck at the Rabbi's outer garment. She's being urged to remain.

The goat cheese woman rolls her small logs of *chèvre* with fine herbs and pepper into a tray for the two hour ride to her goat farm. Flower merchants extend a finger under the beak of the hangers and

27

carry fluttering plants back to their cages in the truck. New York State wine bottles are fitted into compartments by their vintners and driven upstate to the vineyard. Carrots, rutabagas, radishes, beets, parsnips, turnips; all the root vegetables with their soft, clean dirt are going back to the dirt cellar. There is an exodus of machines carrying market leftovers, carcasses of meat, chicken parts, fillets of fish. There is an exodus of people and the sound of traffic is drowned by the twilight twitter of birds, the shiver of trees. One spot of the city belongs to the country and this *Shabbat* we are both before creation and into the busy present. We are walking on the leaves of other autumns, the bones of other citizens.

Behind the trees the Rabbi sees an equestrian statue of George Washington. Competing with it is a woman, atop a soapbox, wearing spectacles and a peculiar flat hat. Her arms are punching the air. Her audience is cheering, "Yeah, Emma." Their voices tinny as the music on an old wind-up Victrola. The scene is the brown of an old rotogravure. The woman is really a young girl and as she speaks her high-pitched voice puts a horse to flight. It is a May Day demonstration. The wind blows. More leaves drift from the trees. the girl is taller, stouter, her eyes milder, but not her words. "Demonstrate before the palaces of the rich. Demand work. If they do not give you work, demand bread. If they deny you both, take bread. It is your sacred duty." Sacred. The Rabbi is attentive to the end of the past century. A hatless, young woman, her hair in a bun, wearing a mini blouse and a dark tie, speaks. "Eight-hour day. Justice for the workers." She is only sixteen and will speak in the square again and again. "Yeah, Gurley." It is Elizabeth Gurley Flynn. "Yeah Gurley," says the crowd and caps fill the air like autumn leaves. The crowd and the ground rumbles under the little Rabbi's feet. Dry autumn leaves jump in the vibration. Under the subway kiosk in slow tread comes the crowd, not speaking, heads bowed. They stand in silence watching the clock. The ground is cold and covered with snow. It is January 1963. When the clock strikes the hour the men remove their hats. They're dead. An American couple sat in chairs, not bridal chairs, not armchairs, but chariots of fire and were consumed. The crowd mourns the Rosen⁄bergs. In silence, the crowd returns to the underground and the earth trembles. "Don't stay," says a voice. The Rabbi jumps. She must have dozed. There's a voice of a miller. He is corking his barrel of hot apple cider. "This will wake you up," he says, handing her a styrofoam cup of the scalding liquid. She sips. "Not in the park after dark," he warns. "It returns to those who had it before or to those who went to capture it now." The rabbi must escape the past to change the future.

❦ Alice Shalvi heads the Israel Women's Network and was principal of Pelech, an experimental religious girls school. She recently retired as professor of English at the Hebrew University in Jerusalem. She spends many months of the year lecturing around the world on topics relating to women and Judaism, and women and Israel.

A L I C E   S H A L V I

Israel Women's Network

The goals and the mandate of the Network are to advance the status of women in Israel in a variety of ways by serving as a lobby or pressure group that attempts to influence lawmakers, mainly men of course, at all levels of government. We want to raise the conscious-ness of the general public, and women in particular, to help us then bring pressure to bear on those who are in power to make women equal partners, equal in status, equal in opportunity, and equal in reward — through legislation or through changes in attitude.

We have been most successful so far in changing attitudes, in bringing the whole issue of women's rights and equality into the public eye. The Network was formed in 1984. The first couple of years were really an up-hill climb: it was very difficult to persuade the media to relate to women's issues which were considered a non-subject. This began to change as demonstrations attracted

31

media attention. An increasing number of women journalists took an interest in the subject, some because they themselves had suffered from discrimination and some because they had changed their opinions. The end result was improved media coverage of women's issues.

We have also had a positive effect on members of the Knesset and ultimately on legislation. The Network has been responsible in effecting major changes in the Knesset since 1986. There was a vital change in the Equal Opportunities in Employment act which extended maternity leave into parental leave. It also included sexual harassment as a form of discrimination in the workplace as a direct result of our lobbying and presentation of working papers to the Knesset. The Network pointed out discriminatory retirement prac⁄ tices in Israel by supporting a woman who was compelled, at the age of sixty, to take retirement. The Equal Retirement Age law was the direct outcome of this test case.

The Network has been successful in raising the issues on every⁄ thing related to divorce or the difficulty of getting a divorce where the husband refuses to give the *get*, the divorce decree. Because we are trying to buck the very deep ingrained religious establishment, we are having some difficulty but the fact that this is something that has come into the public consciousness is very positive. The public was not aware of the extent of the problem.

What is very clear is that we cannot expect to effect major changes in a very short time, but we are getting there. If we just have enough patience and fortitude — it is very hard just to keep slogging away at the same things. It is really like chipping at rocks, but if we hang in there, I think that we will eventually achieve something.

Pelech — an experimental religious school

If I had to point to any one accomplishment in my life which has brought me great enjoyment and satisfaction, it is Pelech School. When the founding principal of the school retired in 1975 I volunteered to take over until we found someone to take the job on a permanent basis. I have been there ever since watching the school grow from forty pupils to over two hundred with twice as many applicants as we can take every year.

I am particularly pleased to see what our alumnae have achieved. These girls are proving that it is possible to exemplify what the school maintains should be the ideal for Israel: a combination of commitment to Judaism, to Zionism, to the Jewish people in Israel or the Diaspora, a commitment to excellence, and the determination to improve society and to devote oneself in some way to making the world a better place. The students take courses not because they need the credits but because they love the studies. Since I have been at the school there have been ten graduating classes. If one wonders whether anything is being achieved, then as my husband keeps pointing out when I am in a state of despair — the very fact that fifty good adults are joining society every year is truly something to be pleased about.

Pelech School has always, since its inception in 1965, taught Talmud to the girls. In that respect it is unlike any other religious high school in the country except for the kibbutz schools. The study of the Talmud, which is completely closed to Orthodox girls in the rest of Israel, stimulates intellectual excitement when it is presented properly, and it certainly sharpens the mind and develops the analytical faculties.

One of the things we are trying to demonstrate is the possibility of fusing Judaism and general studies. In most religious schools the two are separated. The *yeshiva* high schools teach Jewish studies in the morning, secular studies in the afternoon; our claim has always been that we must enable people to integrate the separate parts of their lives into one. A good example is to be found in what we do, or usually do, on the special days we have in connection with most of the holidays. For example, on Hannukah, the feast which cele‑ brates the victory of the Maccabeans over the invaders, we try to get the girls to confront the clash between Hellenism and Hebraism, and then attempt to show how we can integrate both.

Let's take a subject like the conflict between theatre and Judaism — the same conflict that Plato confronted as the artificiality of art which led him to say that art is lying. We then carry on from that to see the way in which our Jewish sages related to art and parti‑ cularly to the theatre as a form of lying and deception. And then continue by considering that we should not cut ourselves off from modern theatre and culture. We want the students to see that things do change and that we have to relate to real problems. We can't say that two thousand years ago the sages said "this is forbidden" and that therefore we have to accept that ban on certain areas of life. We are succeeding in making the girls aware of the real problems of contemporary Jewish life and teaching them that, by working hard, most problems can find a solution and that the solution is firmly anchored in Jewish thought, philosophy, and tradition.

A bat mitzvah story

The difficulty of integrating feminism and Judaism, particularly in contemporary Israel where the two seem to be very separate and sometimes even conflicting, is best illustrated by what happened to me after my first visit to the United States in 1977. I came back to Israel extremely moved and enthusiastic because I had participated quite unintentionally in my first bat mitzvah ceremony in a synagogue just outside San Francisco where I had been the speaker on *Shabbat*. I found myself at a bat mitzvah where not only the girl herself read from the Torah, but her two sisters, her future sister-in-law, her mother, and her grandmother read their own portion of the Torah when they were called up. I was so impressed by these women. They had beautiful voices so that the aesthetic pleasure was enormous and, most important, they were doing something which was unusual even in the United States.

Not all women know how to read from the Torah. When I returned to Pelech I related the story to the whole school and mentioned that I would love to see women more involved in the services and doing similar things in Israel. Well, at that time I had a whole group of very Orthodox male teachers and I was immediately put on the spot by one of them. He said, "I just want to give you a parallel. Suppose in an orchestra the violins started playing the trumpet part or the trumpets started playing the violin part — it would sound terrible! But when everybody, when each instrument plays the part which was written for it, then there is harmony. Right?" Of course, we were supposed to understand what he meant by this.

Unfortunately, or fortunately (I never know how to evaluate this) I, for the first time in Israel, employed a woman Talmud teacher. She was observant but had trained at the Conservative movement's Jewish Theological Seminary in New York because there was, at that time, no Orthodox school at which a woman could train in the Talmud. I asked her — and this compounded the horror — to teach a course for the first time at our school on the status of women in Judaism. The combination of my comments relating to my experience at the bat mitzvah, and this woman teaching that particular course, led ultimately to an enormous crisis in the school. Four male teachers presented me with an ultimatum, "Either she goes or we go." For the next year they made a lot of trouble for me and in the end they left the school.

It seems that this was the crisis Pelech had to go through in order to determine its own identity as a religious feminist school. From this point on we have been moving in a particular direction which not everybody accepts; but the fact that we do have so many applicants shows that it is the kind of school that many parents and their daughters are interested in.

Synagogue experiences

I have had some exciting and important experiences in the synagogue. One of them was the first time I was offered an *aliyah* in the United States in 1979. It was a women's service so it was okay for me to participate, despite my trepidation. When I went up and made the blessing and gazed at the Torah scroll I realized it was the first time in my life — and I was fifty-three years old then — that I had seen the inside of a Torah, and I just burst into tears. I was so overcome by emotion at the realization that while from the age of thirteen this is, or can be, a weekly experience for a Jewish male, it had taken me fifty-three years to be able to experience it.

Another moving experience, and one that caused me considerable anxiety, was when I was the guest speaker at the Spanish and Portuguese synagogue in Montreal, where my good friend Rabbi Howard Joseph is the rabbi. I realized that though it was *Shabbat* morning and the middle of the service, not at the end of the service,

I was expected to speak from the podium right in front of the ark (holding the Torah scrolls) and that, of course, had never happened to me before.

The Spanish and Portuguese synagogue is a very beautiful, majestic synagogue. Norma Joseph came out of the ladies' section with me and we waited by the door. I truly felt more nervous than I did on my wedding day when I think of the enormity of both situations: being called to the Torah and speaking from the rabbi's place before the synagogue congregation in the middle of a proper *Shabbat* prayer service. I felt impelled simply and naturally to make the blessing, *sh'hecheyanu*, that one makes the very first time one does something. These were important moments in my life.

Creating rituals for women

I want my children and grandchildren to realize that Judaism offers valid and important experiences for women as well as for men. Traditional Judaism has been primarily a male experience, at least in public expressions of Judaism: synagogue and ritual. I do not think it is enough simply to join the men. If I say that I was moved being called to the Torah, I think that every woman should be able to have that experience and should not be excluded from it. There are different experiences that women have which I would like to strengthen. In Judaism there is no real expression of a woman's life cycle comparable to the circumcision, the bar mitzvah, the calling up of the bridegroom to the Torah on the Sabbath before or (depending on whether you are Sephardi or Ashkenazi) after the wedding. The Jewish women's movement has been trying to develop rituals for women.

It was one of my happiest moments when I accompanied my oldest daughter, Ditza, the first daughter to get married, to the *mikvah*, the ritual bath, before her marriage. She married into a Kurdish family and the Kurds really make a big ceremony at the bath house. It is a wonderful women's happening where the mother and the aunts of the groom sing a song. They have a set song and set text but they change the details — sort of fill-in-the-blanks: "The bride is Ditza, the daughter of Alice and Moshé" and then they describe the family and the bride. Accompanying my daughter into the *mikvah* and seeing her immerse herself and saying the blessing was absolutely extraordinary. And then there is dancing and singing and special cakes.

The other ritual we as a family began to celebrate was the birth of a daughter. The first occasion to celebrate presented itself when my oldest son had his twins, a boy and girl. So everybody knew we were going to have a *brit milah*, a circumcision. My husband Moshé prepared a beautiful little booklet which outlined a ceremony that we had composed. We selected psalms that were relevant and appropriate both to the occasion and to our family.

When the *brit milah* was over everybody thought, "Okay, this was it," but my son said, "Wait a minute everybody. We have another child. We have a girl baby as well." And we went straight into a naming ceremony for the girl, with my daughter-in-law, the mother of the baby, playing a major role. The most marvellous thing was my daughter-in-law's response. She had had two sons and one daughter before, so she had attended two ritual circumcisions, but this was the first time she had been genuinely involved in a ceremony celebrating the birth of one of her children.

Since that time we have had another grand-daughter and the naming ceremony has become part of the Shalvi tradition.

The past as a key to the future

In Israel we have a law which says that before any building can be erected, archaeologists have to be called in to inspect the foundations to see whether anything of our past history, or other people's past history, can be found. I think the metaphor of delving down before one can erect something new is very appropriate both for Judaism and particularly for Israel. Unless we find what lies behind us in our past, in our tradition, we can never truly create a strong and steady future.

On feminism and political involvement

For me, feminism is equality between the sexes, equality of reward, and equality of status. I think this is what was meant by equality in Israel's Declaration of Independence which said that Israel would be a state based on equality of all citizens, irrespective of race, religion, or gender. I would have thought that was a universal definition. Unfortunately, when most Israeli's hear the word "feminism" they have this very outmoded conception of bra-burning, male-hating women. That is why so many women who really act in a feminist manner, people like Shulamit Aloni or Ora Namir, members of the Knesset who have done a great deal for women's equality in Israel, will say, "I'm not a feminist!" But when you correct them and say, "Oh, don't you believe in everything I have just said?" they say, "Oh, yes. Well if that's feminism, I'm a feminist."

If women were permitted to enter the process of government in Israel and were able to make their personal views on peace part of our government process, we would have a very different political scene in this country. I think that on the whole, women are better at seeking consensus. They are not as confrontational as men are and it is significant that though women have not been active in Israel's political parties they have always been in the vanguard as far as grass-roots movements are concerned. For example, the anti-Lebanese war movement began as Mothers Against Silence, Mothers Against the War in Lebanon, and it was only after the women had started these groups, that men got into the act.

What we have seen in the last year of the Intifada are women's groups very constant in their opposition to government policy. An outstanding example of this is the Women in Black which began as one small group in Jerusalem, then spread to the other cities. As far as I know it is the only group which has been absolutely persistent and consistent in turning up to demonstrate once a week at Paris Square in the centre of Jerusalem. This very regular demonstration effectively makes its point. My feeling is that with more women in mainstream politics we might see something very different in relations with our neighbours.

On feminism and Judaism

My basic feeling about feminism and Judaism is that it should be a process of evolution rather than revolution. I think we can find what one could perhaps call the seeds of a feminist approach even in traditional Judaism. In the summer of 1986 the Network sponsored a dramatic and deeply moving full-day conference at the Knesset on "Women and the Rabbinical Courts." It was a day in which we interwove women telling their own stories with lawyers and jurists who presented possible solutions. Some of the stories were horrendous. One woman, at that time had been waiting twenty-four years for a divorce. Another had been waiting eighteen years. The first woman finally received her divorce after twenty-five years of waiting, the second received hers only recently.

I began that day by telling a story from the Talmud about Rabbi Rachumi. (By the way, the name itself is interesting because the root of the rabbi's name is *rachamim* which means pity or compassion.) Rabbi Rachumi was such a devout scholar that he spent all his time away from home studying. He used to return home only once a year, on Yom Kippur, to visit his wife. Once he did not come. She waited. "He does not come," she said. "He's not coming," she said, and a tear dropped from her eye. At that moment Rachumi went out onto his roof. The roof collapsed beneath him and he died.

Without any further comment, in this succinct manner, the Talmud tells the story. Clearly the moral in the story is that a woman's tears are worth more than a lifetime of Torah study. The tear from the deserted woman's eye counted more with God than the Torah. I used this text to introduce the whole day of the conference, because if the rabbis really heeded the basic meaning of Judaism they could not possibly behave in as uncompassionate manner as they do, without relating to the pain and misery that is involved when a woman is denied the possibility of remarrying or of having more children.

Divorce

In Judaism divorce takes effect not just when a court rules it but when the husband places the Bill of Divorcement in the wife's hands. If the Bill of Divorcement is not given by the husband to the wife, and accepted by the wife, there is no divorce, no matter what the court has ruled. If the husband refuses to give the *get*, the Bill of

Divorcement, or the wife refuses to accept it, that's it, nothing can be done. Women are often in a situation where they need child support and the divorce is more important for them. As long as they are married they cannot set up home with another man. There are very few cases of women holding up the divorce because they want better conditions. However, the man does not have to be divorced in order to set up home or even to have a family with another woman, provided the second woman is not married. In Judaism adultery occurs when a man has a relationship with a married woman. There are now estimated to be ten thousand women in Israel who are waiting for their husbands to grant them a divorce. There are ways to compel a recalcitrant husband to give the *get*. Even the use of physical force is permitted. Unfortunately, the rabbinical courts are not utilizing the tools available to them and we want to make their implementation automatic. We want legislation which says that if the husband still has not given the *get* within six months of the court's divorce ruling, the husband should be automatically jailed. This would avoid a situation where women wait for dozens of years while the rabbinical court decides whether to implement the method it has available to it.

Some feel that until there is also civil marriage and civil divorce in Israel, there will not be adequate competition for the rabbinical system to compel it to reform itself. It is important to bear in mind that reform is possible on a *halalchic* basis, according to Jewish law, and many of us, particularly those of us who are observant Jewish feminists, feel that we don't so much need a wiping out of the religious system as we need Judaism to continue in its traditional way of re/interpreting the law in the light of changing social norms. That is what our great rabbis always did in the past. That is what the rabbinical system in Israel has not done in the past forty years.

Ironically, the rabbinical courts have found solutions for men, in spite of the fact that Israel has a law (passed by the Knesset) against bigamy. There have been over a hundred cases of men being given rabbinical dispensation to take a second wife without being divorced from the first. Of course, this solution is not available for the woman because she is still married. She is not yet unmarried and therefore if she were to marry someone else that would constitute adultery. The fact that the rabbis have seen fit to show compassion for men but have not shown comparable compassion for women is significant.

What underlies this whole problem of personal status is the fact that we do not separate church and state. Perhaps the most pernicious event that has happened in this area was in 1953 when the Knesset invested the rabbinical courts with sole jurisdiction on all issues of personal status. Now, in a way, that also offers hope because the condition that the Knesset bestowed can also be revoked and this could act as a kind of threat upon the rabbinical authorities.

The time has come now to undo this rabbinical authority which constitutes a stranglehold on religious life. It is ironic that we are one of the few countries where the opening session of the Knesset is not accompanied by any kind of prayer or any kind of reading from the scripture. In England this is done and I know that even in the United States, which resolutely separates church from state, a prayer is said in Congress. And yet it does not occur in Israel because religion has become politics. Religion and the State should be separated once and for all.

Feminism in my life

Feminism has served as a powerful binding force in my life. It fuses together many different elements. This is particularly true since I

43

have been teaching women's studies at the university. Now I feel that what I am doing, in every area of my life — whether in my family, at the university, at the school, or at the Network — it is somehow connected with my struggle to bring into existence a more equal and more just society.

Without the enormous support of Moshé, without the sense of partnership in life, I could never have integrated everything in the way he has helped me to integrate it. I have a partner who completely identifies, both in action and in thought, with my own philosophy, though I have not imposed that on him. We have truly grown together into this concept of equality and sharing.

Esther Broner and Alice Shalvi, Jerusalem, 1988

DIALOGUE IN JERUSALEM

❡ This conversation between Alice Shalvi and Esther Broner took place in a Jerusalem café in December, 1988 following the conclusion of the First International Jewish Feminist Conference.

Alice Shalvi & Esther Broner

Alice:

Esther, we have just finished an exhausting three and a half days at the First International Jewish Feminist Conference which, to my mind as an Israeli, started off not altogether correctly with a pre-conference demonstration by the North American delegation on the "Who is a Jew?" issue. The reason I felt fairly strongly that this was a false tactic was because I think it diverted a lot of media and public attention from what I think are different major issues. I know you feel differently but for Israelis the "Who is a Jew?" issue is not really the most vital one at the moment; it is not the issue that relates to most of us.

Esther:

Well there is such a thing as the spontaneous, Alice. Coming over on the plane there was such rage, such anger, and it preceded the conference because it had to be expressed. It wasn't done according to a feminist methodology where it grew out of the conference organically but it was the first of three demonstrations. ('Who is a

45

Jew?' demonstration, 'Women Bringing the Torah to the Wall,' and 'Women in Black.')

Alice:
(Re: Women Bringing the Torah to the Wall demonstration.)
That was already much more central to the Israeli women's experience of having the rabbinical establishment pushing women completely out of public Jewish life and out of spiritual life. By focusing
too much on the "Who is a Jew?" issue I think that ultimately we
did not get the same kind of respect or attention to issues such as the
Leah Shakdiel case, women's role in Jewish public life. The right
of women to sit on all those bodies which relate to issues of rabbinical Jewish law that are so central to our lives, not only for the
Orthodox or observant Jews, but for everybody. I am thinking
particularly of the personal status laws and the need to have women
sitting in the rabbinical courts on the divorce issue.

Esther:
But we gradually became sensitized to that. However, I think there
has to be some respect for our own rage in arriving in Israel and
feeling we are here and already they want to kick out those of us who
have not performed according to their rules of the land. We arrived
with a rage and it had to be expressed. Gradually we were sensitized
to other more specific issues. I think the real issue is the peace issue.

Alice:
I think that the peace issue did come through. One of the strongest
sessions was the women, war and peace session partly because of the
number of speakers from the floor who were expressing a far more
right-wing attitude than we had expected. Perhaps in North America you are more accustomed to very strong divisions on the peace

46

issue but this came as a shock for me and for a number of Israelis that evening.

I realize that the "Who is a Jew?" issue is extremely important for diaspora Jewry and specifically for North American Jewry with its enormous Reform movement. The Reform movement permits conversion without the study and commitment usually required by the Orthodox or even Conservative Judaism and therefore creates Jews who are not considered truly Jewish — in the eyes of the Orthodox rabbinate. But I think there was a danger of the women from North America not really being aware of the extent to which we in Israel fear that politics will be taken over by an ultra-Orthodox element. Ultra-Orthodoxy has as a basis of its tradition simply taken for granted a conception of women which totally excludes them from public life, from ritual, and from Torah learning.

We see examples of this in the last two years, during which, without any kind of legislation, Leah Shakdiel, who was the first Israeli woman elected to sit on a Religious Services Council, was barred from taking her place on that council by the (Orthodox) Minister of the Interior simply vetoing her democratic election to that body. It took two years, including a very costly Supreme Court action (the cost of which, fortunately, was borne by a public body) in order to have her right to sit on that council confirmed. I think that one has to point out that this case does not set a precedent. Any other woman who now gets elected, if there is another woman courageous enough to stand for election, would have to go through the same Supreme Court process.

We had another example of women being barred from sitting on the Electoral Board to choose a new Chief Rabbi of Tel Aviv. These are issues which concern us on a daily ongoing basis more profoundly than the "Who is a Jew?" question.

Israel has a fairly liberal attitude toward abortion. The religious parties demanded that every one of the screening boards which grant permission to abort must include a rabbi who would have veto power. . . .

Esther:
It's sickening, it's sickening!

Alice:
Now this is something which concerns every single Israeli woman, whether she is observant or not.

Esther:
Well, look, the demonstration had to be because people were arriving at the conference with varying degrees of information. Not everybody knew everything . . . .

Alice:
I realize that.

Esther:
I hate to think that one demonstration either wrecked, hurt, or deflected from the conference.

Alice:
Yes I know, but Esther let me make the point that there is a sense among some of us in Israel that North American Jewry almost dictates our agenda.

Esther:
Oh, and we feel the other way. We feel that we are sitting nicely and quietly at home in the U.S. electing a dreadful President and

there is Israel barking and wagging its tail and taking all the attention and doing everything so autonomously — as if we did not exist at all.

Alice:

What was very interesting, actually, was something you just mentioned about North American Jewry's ignorance of what is happening in Israel and also in Europe. I felt that this was a tripartite conference. The North Americans had a very strong contingent and the Israelis very often felt overwhelmed and totally swamped by all the other parties.

Esther:

Well, we came with certain issues to Israel and perhaps the religious issue was important but it was not first on our agenda. It was the peace issue that was first on our agenda and we, as North Americans were reactive, not active, so we have a different view of each other. You think of us as active and I think of us as reactive to Israel having seen all of this dreadful reaction to the Intifada, having viewed this from the United States, our hearts breaking with you. We came very strongly peace-oriented and to truly hear what the Israeli peace women had to say and we could not find them for a long time. They were pretty-well shut out of the conference. In fact we are staying for the post-conference peace event, a speak-out of Israelis and Palestinians which has been separately organized, as if peace is a 'post' issue. So I feel that there were three issues and only some that will organically grow out of the conference.

Alice:

I find it interesting that you call it the peace issue. Most Israelis would define it as the Palestinian issue.

49

Esther:
. . . and probably the Americans also.

Alice:
Okay. I don't know whether one can make such a broad general-ization. I think what shocked some of the more dovish of those among us at this conference, knowing that there were many left-wing American participants (at the session on war and peace which was really a session about the occupation), was the strength and the number of women from the floor who took a distinctly hawkish attitude. This led me to wonder whether we are really correct in our rosy assumption that women are more interested in peace than men are. Perhaps we have built up a false stereotype for ourselves. This is what many of our right-wing sisters in the women's movement keep telling us.

Esther:
That brings out two points. I believe that your hawks packed the session and that some of your people brought their cohorts to pack the gathering.

Alice:
Yes, that's true.

Esther:
To me the paradigm is the Vietnam War twenty-five years ago where there had to be an educational process. Women did go forth in every way at the head of the peace movement. We sat in front of the Induction Boards and we did sit-ins later at the nuclear sites. You also have a very strong and vocal women's peace group that was shut out of this conference. They were not allowed to bring their

issues to the conference and if we deal with the Intifada as a Palestinian issue that to me is defining it only in Israeli terms. I see at as Israeli-Palestinian.

Alice:
Yes, not just peace, it's the nature of the negotiations for many of us — the basis is, what kind of Israel are we going to have?

Esther:
To me the vital session, and the one that was filtered through you my poor dear Alice, was the peace session that you chaired where issues were raised regarding the Intifada.

I am comfortable with dissent, it has happened all my life. We have a paradigm of negotiation and consensus in the women's movement. It was curious to me that an Israeli felt that the American NOW (National Organization of Women) was far left. Where I come from NOW is moderate, centrist, though NOW is, with NARAL, taking on the Pro-Choice fight in the state legislatures and the Supreme Court.

The nub of it to me is that we were all women. Being a woman is risky. Some of the women felt their risk was just being women without attendant problems, but other women felt that the risk was standing in a circle as the "Women in Black" (a group of Israeli and Palestinian women who gather each week to protest the Israeli government's reaction to the Intifada). They were called terrible things and took the brunt of the rage of the populace. In the United States, in support, on Monday nights in New York City, we also join together in front of 515 Park Avenue, where all the major Jewish organizations are located. We stand for an hour and a half. We take abuse. People say to us "Go back to Auschwitz," because we are saying that negotiation is a necessary part of the process.

51

Alice:

You know, this raises a very interesting point because I am very much for demonstration. I think it is very important, at certain times, to stand up and be counted and to make your point publicly. For those of us who are in favour of a two-state solution or finding some other solution to the Palestinian problem which will take into account what has happened in the last forty years during the existence of the State of Israel, the Palestinians, who may have begun as a non-nation, have become a nation, or at least they perceive themselves as such.

For some of us the important action is not so much maintaining a vigil, like the "Women in Black," every Friday, but rather to make our point in an ongoing way. I feel this strongly as an educator because on the morning after the Algiers Declaration in 1988, I, as school principal, as a matter of course felt that after morning prayers, (which is when I have the whole school together), I had to make a statement about this. I had to relate to something that seemed to be a momentous event and so I made a statement saying that I thought something historic had happened and that if the P.L.O. was really prepared to accept our right to safe boundaries and was really ready to make peace, we should welcome the Algiers Declaration.

Esther:

We have had different histories my sweet friend. You have come with great optimism and ideology to make the land and civilize it and I come from a history of dissent, of political discussion in which I almost always found myself in the minority. It is not unusual for me to be in the minority standing on Park Avenue in New York with the "Women in Black." I know I am not being disloyal to Israel. In Israel there seems to be a great sense that you are unpatriotic if you are critical.

Alice:
I think that Americans do feel, (to my mind, incorrectly), that they always have to support Israel, right or wrong — that they have no right to criticize. I do not think that is correct. I perceive Jewry as one entity but any one entity must allow for a pluralistic approach to differences. What has been most painful for us in Israel is that although we have always had an enormous variety of differences, so many political parties, we now have an even greater number of splinter groups. I do not sense ever before having had such a deep-seated division as that between those of us who think that the very nature and future of Israel, particularly its 'moral' future, is at stake here and those who think that this is just another political crisis which we will weather as we have weathered the other wars.

Esther:
I have come from an election in the United States which has caused me to worry about the future of our land in regard to women. I have come to a smaller country where the theocracy is fervent and where your women are going to be shafted as they are in my land. You feel both countries turning into a terribly dangerous direction: militaristic and fundamentalist.

Alice:
In a way it is not even the theocracy that worries me here, so much as the fascism.

Esther:
Yes.

Alice:
We have to distinguish between a very, very dangerous turn to the

right, (in the sense of fascism, totalitarianism, the use of force to solve all differences of opinion) and what we have always had in Israel since the beginning of the State, normally a small minority of religious groups and parties who utilized or exploited their balance-of-power status within the government to extort certain terms in exchange for their participation. What is really dangerous, is that we have rising in our midst a real racism far more overtly expressed now vis-à-vis the Arabs than it has ever been in the forty years of the Jewish State.

Esther:
I know that and it is horrifying but don't forget our last American election was a racist election. In no way were they going to elect a swarthy Greek and his Jewish wife. In no way would the country recognize the Black candidate. It was a taking of the land back for the WASPs. So we have to see it in a more global way.

Alice:
Yes, but your racism, if you call it that, does not involve killing people. Our racism makes it possible for one party to legitimately stand for election though it has as its main platform the proposal to transfer the Arab population from the West Bank in order that Jews should be able to settle there. And this party got two seats in the election.

. In May 1988, just six months after the beginning of the Intifada, I was asked to tour a number of American cities in order to present an Israeli view on the Intifada and to meet and exchange views with women leaders within the Jewish community. One of the things that really horrified me was the extent to which many of the women felt that they had to support the Israeli government because otherwise they would be perceived as being disloyal to Israel. I remember clearly the effort of conveying to them that there is a diversity of views in Israel, that it is not one monolithic entity, any more than any other community or state is. I wanted them to know that it was important that they support those of us in Israel who were desperately going against the general tide of greater extremism which always grows whenever one encounters violence on the other side. What we are seeing is a terrible, vicious cycle of one side escalating force and the other side, in its turn, feeling the need to use greater force. World Jewry feel that they have to support the Government's position even when it is one which many of us in Israel fear will lead us into disaster.

❡ *Michele Landsberg is the bestselling author of* Women and Children First *and* This is New York, Honey. *She writes a regular column for the* Toronto Star *and has won two National Newspaper Awards. Michele is involved in the New Israel Fund to support women's causes in Israel, and is spearheading a Jewish feminist network in Toronto.*

MICHELE LANDSBERG

Childhood and family

I came to my present position on Judaism by a long, muddled, and continuous search. As far back as I can trace it began when I was about four years old and my mother was politely trying to explain to me about God. I distinctly remember standing there and listening to my mother, whom I adored, explaining to me that there was a God and I was thinking, "Why does Mommy believe this silly, patently false thing?"

My mother was in the Reform congregation in Toronto, Holy Blossom Temple. I was brought up there in a sort of bloodless, feeling-less modernism that never meant a thing to me. I was sent to the religious school there from the time I was four until I was fifteen or sixteen. The entire class was graduated in a group ceremony in the synagogue — "Confirmation" it was called. We were dressed in white robes, held flowers, put on lipstick to look pretty for the photographs and got blessed by the rabbi. It was a completely meaningless event to me.

The whole time I was at Holy Blossom I was an outsider. The congregation was wealthy and extremely materialistic. This was immediately after the post-war period and our family was not wealthy. We did not even live in the neighbourhood and I was reminded of that constantly by the other students. I was also a little budding intellectual — I wrote poetry passionately. I cared about ideas and there were so few people at Holy Blossom who seemed to share that with me. They were fixated on appearances and possessions and I knew I did not belong there, but then where did I belong?

Once at Simchat Torah, my grandpa took me down to the little Orthodox *shul* that he had built. He was a carpenter. We went downtown and I remember the tumult and the strange, little, old men. They were eating chickpeas outside and there was commotion — there was life, vibrant life. They were dancing around with the Torahs and I got to hold an apple with a candle on top of a little flag. Yet I knew that despite the excitement that was not my place either.

I thought I had found my place when I joined the Labour Zionist movement as a young teenager. That seemed to be a good thing because everyone was against it. Holy Blossom went berserk with outrage that I was a Zionist. Zionism is so accepted, so established in the Jewish community now. People forget that Reform and Orthodox Jews were very anti-Zionist in the days before the formation of the State of Israel. The rabbi was delegated to convince me not to be a Zionist. That didn't work. The Director of Education set about the task — some of his warnings come back to me now with heart-breaking prescience. He was a marvellous, cynical, bitter man from Germany and he used to tell me that the Zionist youth movement was just "seduction and games" and he had dire forewarnings of what Israel would one day become. He did not convince me and I felt I was truly at home. I was with other youngsters who cared about Jewish identity and had a Jewish identity that was neither Orthodox, in a way I could not accept, nor this bland, conformist, materialistic, meaningless Reform.

We had a gentile choir at Holy Blossom, and an organ throbbing Christianly throughout our services. Everything was in English — there was no Hebrew. Luckily, the Zionist movement taught me Hebrew, customs, and holiday traditions, so I was equipped to raise my children with some sense of Jewish identity.

There was no congregation, no group that I could fit into. I was a politically active left-wing person with convictions about feminism and a deep sense of solidarity with the Jewish people. Where did that fit in Toronto? Nowhere! I could not find like-minded people anywhere.

I decided to make my own Jewish celebrations at home for the children. We had wonderful Purim carnivals, seders for Passover. I learned from books how to do *havdalah*, the service ending the sabbath. I learned all that stuff either from books or my memories of the Zionist movement and tried to make Jewishness the full, rich, living, human, celebratory experience that it had not been for me in my childhood.

My mother was really of the shell-shocked generation. I think the Jewish community in Canada came out of the Second World War stunned and speechless. My mother's idea was: "Don't get them mad. Keep quiet. Be Jewish but don't look different. Don't act different." There was also a deep, deep silence about the Holocaust. It was never spoken of, certainly not at Holy Blossom. We were "passing for white" in Canada and, of course, for a thinking and passionate youngster, that is not good enough. The form of Judaism that my mother tried to practice, something that would be neutral enough not to alienate us from Canada but Jewish enough to keep us tied to the community, did not work.

I was a real rebel, a spitfire. When I was about fourteen the only way I could get home from Zionist meetings downtown to our house in the suburbs was by hitch-hiking. Once when I was hitch-hiking home the police told me to stop. I refused because it did not seem rational to me — there was no other way to get home. They picked me up and took me to the police station where I refused to identify myself — the new rebellion of a fourteen year-old. From a Holy Blossom library book I had with me the police deduced I was a member of the congregation and they sent a police cruiser to pick up Rabbi Abraham Feinberg to identify me. Rabbi Feinberg posed as a great liberal — open-minded and tolerant. My working mother, poor, struggling to make it and to be genteel, thought she was so much part of this congregation. When Rabbi Feinberg was brought to the police station he was furious and he hissed at me, "How do you think it looks for a police cruiser to come to my house?" And then he turned to the police and said, "Well, you know, she's rather a difficult youngster. Her mother works." And iron entered my soul at that moment because I saw instantly how my mother was more or less ostracized by so many of the wealthy people in the congregation and, indeed, by the rabbi, because she worked for a living.

Spirituality and belief

When I met Esther Broner and the Seder Sisters after I moved to New York it was really the first time I even allowed myself to play with some of those ideas of spirituality and belief. All my religious

observance through Darchei Noam, the Reconstructionist congregation, have been tribal solidarity — feeling part of a community
and a tradition, loving to sing the Hebrew songs. However, religion
in itself and religious belief is something very foreign to me. Because
Esther Broner and the other women were creating new ways that
were inclusive of women, embracing women and women's experience and our ties to our children and to the rest of the world, for the
first time I thought, well, I love and honour these women, I'll enter
into the spirit of this thing. I do not know how far I have come with
it but I am willing to respect it and take part in it because of my
regard for these women and their integrity.

Spirituality is so open to abuse and easy answers. I see so much
silliness in the New Age consciousness. I guess I am a rationalist.
I am a believer in political principles, in history, and in as rigorous
thought as I can bring myself to, but not in fuzzy spirituality and
mysticism. A retreat into mystical belief makes me intensely uncomfortable. I see it as a way to evade the basic questions of justice and
of how to live decently together in this world. The new rituals Esther
Broner is working out are an expression of Jewish feminism in
which I can participate in with ease.

A Purim story

The Jewish stories and legends we learned as youngsters at Holy
Blossom Religious School had so little space for girls or women. I
remember my indignation and bewilderment about the Purim
story.

Everyone loves Purim, right? But there was Queen Vashti, of
whom we know so little. Ahashuerus, king of Persia and Media,

demanded that she perform a dance before assembled guests and notables at a banquet. She refused and was dismissed. The Purim story depicts her as a villainess. Then Esther was chosen to be queen in a beauty contest: docile, beautiful, submissive Esther. She was the good one in the story — she saved the Jewish people.

Saving the Jewish people was important but at the same time her whole submissive, secretive, manipulative way of being was the absolute archetype of 1950s womanhood. It repelled me. I thought, "Hey, what was wrong with Vashti? She had dignity. She had self-respect." She said, "I'm not going to dance for you and your pals." There I was, nine or ten years old, and I thought, "I like Vashti but I'm supposed to hate her." Puzzling.

Segregating women

When I was eighteen and in Israel, our group from the Institute for Youth Leaders was taken to the Mea Shearim section of Jerusalem for Simchat Torah. To my surprise the girls were led up a narrow, filthy backstairs to a small, miserable, dirty, cold room. We were told, "If you look through this hole in the wall you can watch the men celebrating the Torah." I was filled with fury and contempt for these men whose pride had to come from degrading women. I vowed that I would never again enter a segregated institution. I already had strong feelings about black/white segregation; now I had very strong feelings about man/woman segregation.

I never did go into a segregated institution again until Esther was mourning her father's death and she decided to honour him by saying *kaddish* every day in a little, Orthodox neighbourhood *shul*. I had mourned my mother and I know how strong is the urge to mourn your parent in the most Jewish way, in the way that would do them the most honour. I really felt that what Esther was doing was noble and for her sake I went with her. I saw how the women were crowded onto the end of the bench behind a plastic shower curtain — such a fitting symbol, it seemed to me, of the sleaziness of the tradition of segregating the women from the men. The men arrogated to themselves all the space on the bench and the little left over at the end was for any women who would be kept hidden away.

I loathe this tradition and it was hard for me to sit there behind the curtain with Esther but at the same time there were ten or twelve of us friends who went with her. We felt weirdly powerful. We felt that the men were afraid of us — and they were. What did they fear so much? To be in contact with women? It was not an entirely negative experience. We felt somehow exultant just being there together. The men were all on the defensive. I think they knew that it was a rotten tradition they were enforcing and were ashamed of what they were doing. I am not sure they were ashamed but I think they did not want us to be in the *shul* to see what their custom was. If they were not ashamed then I despise them all the more for it. I do not believe in upholding two thousand year-old traditions that are discriminatory and filled with contempt for the other sex; you are not enhancing Judaism or preserving anything except a kind of primitive gesture.

I always wondered how the Orthodox women whom I deeply respect — women of integrity and intelligence — how can they be subject to such discrimination? How can they allow themselves to be so degraded, to be hived off into some segregated gallery or separate part of the *shul*?

The whole time I was growing up at Holy Blossom there was the pretension of it being so modern, but women were never on the *bimah*; women never carried the Torah; women did not have Bat

63

Mitzvahs. The first time I ever touched the Torah was when I was called up on my daughter's Bat Mitzvah. It was a thrilling moment and my children laugh at me because I am so filled with emotion whenever, for example, my youngest daughter Jenny parades with the Torah during services at the Darchei Noam. The Torah is sacred to me even though I am not religious. I cannot explain these contradictions but I am a Jew and the Torah is powerful. When Jenny parades by carrying the Torah with her eyes bright, she always warns me ahead of time, "Mom, don't cry." But I can't help it because it is such a strong moment for me, such a moment of affirmation. For me there are all those old feelings of having been forbidden, rejected, and deprived so that tears come to my eyes when I talk about touching the Torah. For Jenny it is just part of being a human being.

A positive synagogue experience

When I joined the Reconstructionist congregation, Darchei Noam, I was delighted by the way the voices of the men and women were raised together. Traditionally women were silent in the synagogue; you never heard their voices except when they were serving tea and cookies afterwards or when they were scolding the children along to the nursery school.

It was tremendously moving moment when Phyllis Angel Greenberg sang *Kol Nidre* in a lovely, tender, and passionate voice — a voice filled with womanly understanding. There was not a dry eye in the synagogue — we were all terribly moved. For my family this is the highlight of the year.

Sometimes I worry about whether much of feminism is a kind of egotism thrusting ourselves forward as the Orthodox accuse us of doing. Sure, we want to be first and foremost [equal with men?]. . . . On the other hand I see it as a lovely blending of voices. A male voice alone is not humanity for me. It is the blending of voices, male and female, children's and adult voices, that together make a whole human sound.

On Orthodoxy

Whenever I used to celebrate *havdalah* with the children I would pay attention to the words, making a difference between light and dark, between the sabbath and the other days, between Jews and non-Jews. I believe in that. I do not think Orthodoxy is the way. Orthodoxy is driving differences between Jews and alienating many thousands of us.

I grew up in a home that believed in assimilating on the surface and this resulted in my two older brothers marrying non-Jews. All their children are non-Jews and the generations that follow are lost to the Jewish people. I think that is a terrible loss. Jewish history is precious and rich and has given so much to the world and I do not want it to be diluted, although I do not think it is a wholly, religious history and tradition. There is much more to it than that. That is what we modern and Reconstructionist Jews are involved with: trying to work out how we can be part of the modern world, but still Jews, and not totally assimilated. I have struggles with this with my own children. The question of inter-marriage comes up over and over again. They have mostly non-Jewish friends and I do not want them to inter-marry. I do not want them to be lost to Jewish-ness, to lose their identity and all that is precious in that. It is not because I think Jews are precious in themselves; it is because we have given the world so much and we can give so much more. How do you maintain that delicate boundary that is constantly shifting in the modern world? This is something I struggle with week in, week out, and I do not have an answer.

Becoming a feminist

I think that being Jewish did, in a way, spawn my feminism because you were always an outsider growing up Jewish in Toronto in the 1940s. An outsider is critical, aware. You ask questions, challenging received opinions. While the whole world is singing "Jesus loves me, yes I know" in kindergarten, you know that you are not supposed to be singing it so you have time to think about why and what makes you different.

I grew up questioning male and female roles too. They were equally rigid and pre-defined and by the time I was eleven or twelve I was challenging and rejecting them. Perhaps if I had not grown up Jewish I would not have been a feminist. I was certainly a feminist long before any of my friends. When I got to university in 1958 I could not find anyone else who shared my concerns about injustice to women. No one. I was all alone but that did not stop me. I went right on feeling as strongly and announcing my ideas as strongly as possible but it was not until the early 1960s that the Women's Movement came along. I felt that my whole stance as a Jew who was somehow marginal to society was very much like my stance as a woman. So the two of them are intertwined in my mind.

Did feminism enrich my Judaism? There is no question about that. I found my way back to a form of Judaism that satisfies me as much as it can be and gives me a context. I found an egalitarian congregation that includes women instead of rejecting them and

66

now I feel more Jewish and more committed than ever. And now, I'm even more deeply linked to the women of the Feminist Seder. This has enhanced and deepened my feeling of belonging to Judaism.

One of the great tragedies is that traditional Judaism was so smug, so negligent, and so callous towards its women. It took these feminists, strong and wonderful women for granted; dismissed their claims to full participation, and lost them. Almost all the leaders of the feminist movement in North America were Jewish. They accomplished wonders for women but they did not identify themselves as Jews because they were alienated from smug Establishment Judaism. I think this is a crime and a terrible loss for Judaism. I see the Seder Sisters as women who are creatively struggling to make a space in Judaism for women. The traditionalists may not yet welcome this gift, but one day we will re-nurture Judaism so that it becomes more whole.

My vision is that we will go on creating our own rituals, our own experimental reaching out forms of Judaism and at the same time we will bring that to both genders; that will become part of the ongoing life of Judaism. I think that we do need our separate experiences now to heal the wounds of having been excluded for so many centuries. Yet I am very suspicious of segregationist streams. I believe that an all woman form of Judaism could be as barren, arrogant, and sterile as the male-dominated form that has been practiced. I want to see the two come together and I see our separate women's endeavours as being a little tributary that will add to the flow of the greater stream eventually. As for the future, if Judaism is too rigid and formalized to accept this new stream of thought and experience coming from women, then it will be simply amputating its living parts, cease being a creative and living force, and become a relic.

Michele Landsberg's daughter Ilana Lewis (back row centre), Michele Landsberg, and Esther Broner join the "Women in Black" in Jerusalem.

Israeli politics

After the Israeli elections of 1988, I was appalled and heart-broken by the grip the ultra Orthodox party had on the whole electoral process. The *Toronto Star* ran a story listing the demands of the religious parties in Israel. Number one: no women in the Cabinet. Number two: no abortion. It was clear that the agenda of the right-wing was to dominate and control women. It was almost their *raison d'être*. It was so clear to me that this was happening to the country I love and am loyal to, that in my fury and horror I decided I would not go to the Empowerment of Women Conference taking place in Jerusalem in the fall of 1988. My heart was broken — I felt I could not go to Israel. Then I thought about the Israeli women, the feminists, who were fighting the good fight, isolated and experiencing difficult times. Perhaps they could use some support from Jews in the Diaspora like me. I decided to go.

Re-visiting Israel after thirty years, listening to the complacency and sentimentalism of some of the North American women, and the narrow ranting bigotries of some of the right-wing Israeli women only deepened my sense of estrangement and despair.

68

Politics

Politics is my *halacha*, it is my law of being, of how to live. Politics is inherent in everything we as a family do and how we live; whether you cheat on your income tax or not, whether you take profit from the sale of land or not. Our belief in democratic socialism and in a fairer, more just and compassionate world guides us in our daily life, possibly in the same way that Jewish law guides the Orthodox.

I became political when I was eighteen and on a kibbutz in Israel. I suddenly realized that this was the right way to be — money is not the measure of everything. Cooperation and caring for each other is more productive. When I returned to Canada I translated that into a commitment to the New Democratic Party and I have been active in the party my entire adult life. All three of my children too. Of course, my husband was an active politician for many years but we absolutely shared that; to me it is the same kind of ethical commitment that Judaism is. We had many little rules in the family which demonstrated this. At the dinner table the littlest would always be served first and the other children would say, "Why?" Whether or not it appeared in the Talmud I said, "That's a Jewish rule. You feed the animals first because they are the most helpless and most dependent on you, then the servants, the children, and only then the adults." This seems right to me. It is the right hierarchy of care and concern. Jewishness and Democratic Socialism are so intertwined that I cannot separate them. They are all one way of being to me — Israel was a socialist country and that was part of the Zionist dream. I have been heart-broken for years as Orthodox fanaticism increases in Israel and North-American capitalism, greed, and self-interest works its way into the Israeli political system.

¶ Elyse Goldstein is a rabbi. She is presently director of Kollel — *A Centre for Liberal Jewish Learning in Toronto. Many of her articles on women and Judaism have been published in Jewish and secular periodicals. She is chair of the Reform Jewish Practices Committee of the Central Conference of American Rabbis, and is a member of the board of Mazon Canada — a Jewish organization dedicated to fighting hunger.*

RABBI ELYSE GOLDSTEIN

Becoming a rabbi

The journey to become a rabbi started when I was twelve or thirteen years old, when I was in Hebrew school. I was the only girl in my class so naturally all my teachers gave me a lot of attention. It was a very special time for me.

When I entered my teenage years I decided I wanted to do something in the Jewish community; be a leader of some sort, and I looked for a role model.

What were women doing in my community? The most active role model I could find, of course, was the rabbi's wife, the rebbitsen. The rebbitsen in the community where I grew up was very active. She was learned, involved, and also very beautiful. At age sixteen I said, "That's what I want to be." So for a long time I thought that my course of action was to marry a rabbi. Of course things did not work out that way. I did get married but my husband became my rebbitsen.

When I was seventeen I met one of the first women to study in a rabbinical school to become a rabbi. I looked at her and I said, "Oh, my God, I don't have to be the rebbitsen, I can be the rabbi!" And ever since then the path was straight-forward for me.

Rabbinical school was an interesting experience for me. A third of my class were women and they were very vocal. We changed the language of liturgy when it was our turn to lead services for the school. We challenged our professors to find texts about women for us to study. We pressed for the hiring of women faculty. One of the old school professors whom I remember fondly would start every class with, "Good morning, gentlemen," even though there were seven women in the room.

We also received advice. In my senior year as we were about to go and be interviewed for positions, one of the professors called us together and said, "You know, you should play down the women's things you've done in the school. You don't want people to think you are only a rabbi for women. You should not make a big deal out of the feminist things that you have published or the feminist groups that you have lead or the women's studies that you have done as a student. You should really say that you're a rabbi for all people." Of course, most of smiled and said, "We understand where you are coming from," and then went on to our interviews. I never played down my involvement in women's causes and the word 'feminist' actually appeared on my resumé. A lot of people were frightened by that.

One of my favourite stories about my early experiences as a woman in the rabbinate was when I was still in school. I was asked to come back to my home congregation where I grew up to read from the Torah scroll on the High Holidays. No woman had ever done that in my congregation before and I practiced for weeks. I was a perfectionist. I knew that I had to do this perfectly because while I was up there reading from the Torah, every woman in the world was up there with me. If I did it badly, they would never ask another woman again. I practiced and I worried until the big day came. I got up and chanted from the Torah flawlessly. You could hear a pin drop. When I was finished people came forward on the reception line to congratulate me — they all said how wonderful I was. Then an old man walked up to me, a man I had known since I was a child, and he said to me, "You know Elyse, I must tell you. You did a wonderful job but the truth is I didn't hear a word you chanted." And I asked him, "Why not? Was I not loud enough? Did I make a mistake?" "No," he said. "I didn't hear a word you chanted because I couldn't listen — I was watching your beautiful legs the whole time!" It was hard for me to hear that.

Studying and taking the title of rabbi was a very radical act. It was getting what was rightfully mine, something that had been denied women over the centuries. It made me think of all the women who functioned as rabbis throughout Jewish history but were denied the honour of the title. When I walked down the aisle of Temple Emmanuel and became ordained, I was overwhelmed with the feeling that not only was I being ordained but that women who had been denied the title of rabbi were receiving it as well. It is very empowering for me to think that I am fulfilling a role in honour of so many women.

It is also extremely exciting for me to step down from the *bimah*, the pulpit, and have women approach me and say, "Seeing you up there has taught me that I can do it, that I can take a leadership role in the community, that my voice can be heard." And it is an important experience for men to participate in a congregation where a woman is leading the congregation in prayer, giving a sermon, or reading from the Torah. It teaches men and boys an important lesson: there is room, and there must be room for women to take positions of leadership in the community.

Rabbi Elyse Goldstein at the baby naming ceremony of Sarah, daughter of co-director Roushell Goldstein, Toronto, May 1988.

RABBI ELYSE GOLDSTEIN
℘ *Ordination blues*

They say that rabbis all have beards,
They say that rabbis all talk low,
They say that rabbis bring out tears
They look at me and they all say "NO."
I got the sacred pains, ain't it a shame
I want to be ordained blues
I got the sacred pains, ain't it a shame
I want to be ordained blues.

Walking down 110th Street,
I'm looking for a school that'll take me in
They say, "We'll let you start your studies
but to give you ordination would be a sin,"
I got the sacred pains, ain't it a shame
I want to be ordained blues
I got the sacred pains, ain't it a shame
I want to be ordained blues.

But we go to school, follow all their rules,
"Don't bitch, don't snitch, don't ever cry,"
Learn the cases, kiss the right places
Looking for a job? They just pass us by.
I got the sacred pain, ain't it a shame
I want to be ordained blues
I got the sacred pains, ain't it a shame
I want to be ordained blues.

Not tall enough, not old enough,
If I'm dressing down I'm not bold enough
If I'm talking loud, I'm not soft enough
I guess I'm just made of the female stuff.
I've got the sacred pain, ain't it a shame
I want to be ordained blues
I've got those sacred pains, ain't it a shame
I want to be ordained blues.

The men in school all try and act cool,
"Oh we're not threatened, we don't want to fight,
We like our women equal in *shul*";
But just try and get a date on a Saturday night!
I've got those sacred pains, ain't it a shame
I want to be ordained blues
I've got those sacred pains, ain't it a shame
I want to be ordained blues.

What sect you're in doesn't matter much,
They say, "Give us time. We still need to see,"
But we know that change ain't in a rush
As long as He who does the teaching and
He who does the preaching and He who names
the child, and He who knows the Bible, and
He who runs the school, and He who writes
the rules, and He who calls the hour, and
He who has the power is not a She.
I've got those sacred pains, ain't it a shame
I want to be ordained blues
I've got those sacred pains, ain't is a shame
I want to be ordained,
I want to be ordained, blues.

At the time I wrote the song "Ordination Blues" the Jewish Theological Seminary, which is the conservative, rabbinical seminary (near 110th Street), had not yet opened its doors to women who wanted to become rabbis. I knew many wonderful, talented, skilled women who wished to be conservative rabbis. I thought there had to be a way for me to share their pain and anguish with the community. "I am a leader, a spokesperson, I'll write a fire and brimstone sermon and give it out from every pulpit in the land," I said to myself. I decided, instead, to treat the subject with humour and so I wrote the song. I have sung it (and I am not a musician) and used it as a humorous way to get people to listen to the issue — there are women out there who want to be Reform, Conservative, *and* Orthodox rabbis. They don't want to move to another community. They want to be in their own communities and they've got the blues.

Linking Judaism and feminism

We have several options when we are faced with the patriarchal nature of Judaism. We can give it up and say, "You know, the religion is simply too patriarchal. I can't deal with it, I'm leaving." And some women have taken that option. It is a sad option because it makes our community lose some of its best talents and its strength. The alternative is to say, "Isn't there something already within our tradition that I can rediscover, that I can pick up and make my own." I think that is what I do as a Jewish feminist. I look within the Torah, for example, at the matriarchs. Is there something they can teach me about women in Judaism. I look at the Talmud and I might look at Bruriah as a role model. I look at women as leaders and learners in the community. Is there something I can learn from them?

Most of all it is in theology that I find great strength and a synthesis between Judaism and feminism. Within the Jewish framework and our tradition there are many feminine images of God, one of which is the *shekinah*, God as the female presence of the universe, the mothering presence, the creative force. Another image is the *harachaman* which comes from the root *rechem*, meaning 'womb.' Can you imagine standing up in a synagogue and saying, "Oh, Womb of the Universe." That is what I do occasionally and sometimes people are shocked but it stimulates them to see the link between Judaism and feminism. The way that I try and live my life both as a Jew and a feminist is to find the voices that have been silenced through the centuries, to give women their voices back, to hear what those women are saying to me and to hear what the feminine image of God might be saying to me. There are great possibilities in Judaism if we do not cast it aside and say there is nothing salvageable in it. There are still many aspects of the tradition that speak to us as women.

The next generation

When I think about the next generation I think about how blessed they are. They are so fortunate to be able to look up at the *bimah* of a synagogue and see women up there; not only a woman rabbi but women getting an *aliyah*, called up to the Torah, women reading from the Torah and taking leadership roles.

I think of myself as a twelve year-old girl, sitting in the congregation looking up at the *bimah* and saying, "I want to be up there one day," and never knowing it was possible. All the girls and boys in my congregation now look up and see that it is possible. They observe their mothers and their sisters and know that the leader of the congregation is a woman.

When I tutor children for their bat mitzvah and bar mitzvah we discuss the Torah portions they are studying. If there is a woman in a certain Torah portion I ask them how they feel about this. How does it make them feel, as a girl or as a boy, to learn about this matriarch? If something comes up about women in the religious text or in the actual subject I am teaching, students will often raise their hands and say, "You know, I never thought of that before, but now having a woman rabbi I'm aware that there is an issue of women in the text or even an absence of women in the text."

Children are now fortunate to have role models. Jewish children, particularly girls, know that it is possible to be anything they want to be in the Jewish community today. No one can stand in their way any more. In the secular world they can become doctors, lawyers, whatever they want. When children enter the synagogue I want them to feel they can do anything they want in the Jewish world too. It is very exciting to be part of this process.

Feminism and men

It is imperative that feminism include men. First of all we share the world with them and they are fifty percent of the population. When men deal with feminists they are opened up to a whole new world, a totally new way of looking at the world: different eyes for reading the text, different ears to hear the songs being sung, different hearts to feel the emotions of both pain and joy that women feel. We have to share that experience with men and enrich them as much as they enrich us. Should we be separatist? Should we say that we are going to form our own community of women and make that our own separate little space? I believe we must be inclusive of men because we so much need each other in this endeavour.

79

The following is a good example. I study every week with a male colleague in town, another reform rabbi. He is my *chavrusah*, my study partner, and just a few weeks ago we were studying from the *Mishna Torah* — a compilation of Jewish laws by Maimonides. We were studying the laws regarding what would be considered forced intercourse. One of the things we noticed in the course of that study was a tendency in the text to assume that women are accustomed to being forced sexually, that they might even come to expect it as a natural outcome of sexuality. All of a sudden my male colleague stopped me and said, "Wait a minute. Had I been studying this text with a man I think I would have turned the page and continued to the next section of text without even stopping to think about what a woman might be thinking or feeling by hearing this text." He continued, "Let's stop. I want you, as a woman, to tell me how this text affects you. Where is your pain? What does it say to you about being a woman and a sexual being in this religious tradition?" We stopped, and the rest of our study session dealt with my pain; my response to that text; what it said to me as a woman; and the assumption that women might have to be forced into sexual inter-course as a natural outcome of being female. My colleague stated over and over again to me that he had never heard those kind of voices in the text before when he studied with men. And he hoped that other male colleagues would study the text with women so they could see the text with different eyes.

Egalitarianism

There is room for both egalitarianism and feminism within the community. It is important to have ceremonies or rituals in which men and women participate equally, where the symbols used are

both male and female. An example might be a *brit milah*, a circumcision, where traditionally it has been very male-oriented language
with just the father present and the other men who have made a
minyan. The mother has been shunted off into another room. Equality can be established in the ceremony by bringing women into it
and by making the language of the ceremony more egalitarian.

Then there is the feminist side — rituals for women by women:
baby-naming rituals, menstrual rituals, rituals for weaning a child
or rituals that talk to women about the cycles of her own life. There
may be a calling for these rituals to be women-centred or women-
focused. Whether or not men will be part of them depends on the
future because these rituals are so new. Most of them are creative and
experimental. I think it is possible for men and women to be
involved in egalitarian ceremonies. At the same time I think it is fair
and reasonable to say that women can have a separate space to
experiment with things that have not been done before for themselves.

New rituals

There are two ways to look at the question of life cycle ceremonies
for women. The first is: where can we fit ourselves into the existing
structures such as baby-namings, where there had been, in the past,
only *brit* (circumcision) ceremonies for boys. How can we enrich
the experience of bat mitzvahs for girls when there has been a bar
mitzvah for boys? Can women take a more active role in the Jewish
wedding ceremony where they have been passive? These are basically acceptable and non-threatening to the establishment. The
second more challenging, and ultimately more important question,
concerns those life experiences of women that have never been

addressed above and beyond having a baby. The moment of actual birth — what does the mother say, what can she do that is spiritual? What about weaning ceremonies; ceremonies when children leave the house; and ceremonies for menstruation? Menstruation, probably the most significant physical event in a woman's life, virtually goes unnoticed. What about ceremonies that have to do with women's psyches, with women's spirituality? What about naming female images, like the moon? We do have a Rosh Chodesh, New Moon celebration, but it really is not understood and is not part of the regular Jewish cycle of events. It is not perceived as being in the mainstream of Jewish activities. I would like to see women put themselves into what is existing but as Jewish feminists what we really need to do is to name and create ceremonies for those experiences in women's lives that have been ignored, ritually, until now.

A ritual reappraised

The *mikvah* is a ritual bath where women traditionally would go to cleanse and purify themselves after their menstrual cycle. Following this *mikvah* women were then allowed to resume sexual activity with their husbands.

Mikvah is one of my favourite experiences and I feel like I am reappropriating it. I am going for different reasons than tradition would normally dictate for women. I go on Rosh Chodesh to celebrate the new moon. I have gone to the *mikvah* with my friends who are infertile and could not bear children. I have done ceremonies with them in the water to give them strength to get through their barrenness. I have gone to the *mikvah* for celebrations of fortieth birthdays, mid-life crises, all sorts of things. I do not see the *mikvah* only as a place where women go at the end of their menstrual cycle to be able to have sex with their husbands afterwards. I do not see it as permission to go forth to men. I see it as an inward permission to be who you are, to be fully female, to experience your own cycle.

The most wonderful experience I have ever had in the *mikvah* was when I was a bride. I took six of my favourite and best female friends to the *mikvah* with me and I guess you would have to say we stormed the *mikvah*. We ran in singing songs. The *mikvah* is usually quite reserved — the women don't want to make a big fuss about being there. Well we came in with tambourines, chanting and singing our bridal songs and my friends proclaimed, "We have a bride!" and they brought me into the *mikvah*. First I did the ritual 'kosher style' and then all five of my girlfriends took off their clothes and jumped into the *mikvah* with me. Each one of them gave me blessings and then would dunk me; and this went on for about an hour. Finally the *shomerit*, the woman in charge, said, "This is really a bit too much. I have never seen anything like this before," and she ordered us out. Subsequently I wrote an article about this experience to share it with women who are afraid to go to the *mikvah* because they think it is not for modern women — for feminists. It is, but you have to take it and give your own meaning, a feminist meaning. The *mikvah* is a good example of taking something that women have thought of as a negative image and turning into a positive one.

Changing the image of God

Looking at women as authority figures has forced men to be humbled, to know that power has to be shared and this has been one of feminism's great benefits for the Jewish community. The following is an example.

83

When you are praying to God only in male-oriented language
— he, father, king, etc. — as a male growing up you come to
understand that godliness is next to maleness, that it really is a
corollary. If I want to be like God I have to be 'father-king' strong.
Changing the image of God and therefore changing the authority
figures has also opened men up to a gentler stream within themselves
and within Judaism. If God can be compassionate, mothering,
loving, and nurturing then certainly men can be the same. We have
a different image and different role model of God.

We know that the endeavour of Judaism is to be like God. If we
want to be like God and we are women, perhaps God has to be
more womanlike. That also brings a whole sense of gentleness into
one's life outside of Judaism. If we are going to share power within
Judaism, share responsibility, and are going to be nurturing and
strong, then we also take that, hopefully, into our lives at home and
in the workplace. It will also affect how you are going to raise your
children. Children growing up now are going to see mothers and
fathers participating equally in rites that used to be for the fathers
only and they are going to view the world differently as well. Boys
and girls can do many more things than the little boxes and cate-
gories we have put them in for so many hundreds of years.

Role models

There are so many wonderful role models within Judaism which
prove to me that you can be a feminist within the Jewish tradition.

In the Torah (Parshat Pinchas — Numbers 27) there were the
daughters of Zelophehad whose father died. He had no sons.
According to the biblical law of inheritance at this time, only sons
could inherit. These brave daughters went to Moses with a very

reasonable claim. Since they had no brothers why should their father's land be given to somebody else? Why couldn't the daughters inherit it? Moses listens and agrees it is a good question and decided to find out the answer.

This is the most significant story in the Torah for me. Moses goes and asks God, "What's proper here?" And God says, "The daughters of Zelophehad are right! Let them inherit." This is an excellent example of women getting that which is theirs to have.

Outside of the books of the Torah and the other books of the Bible for role models I think of women like Vashti in the apocryphal Book of Esther. In this Purim story she refused to dance naked in front of the King and his drunk courtiers. She was punished for her refusal and lost the title of Queen. She was replaced with Queen Esther, another good role model: a woman who, within the constraints of being female at that time, used her "wiles" to save the Jews. But I like Vashti better — she is more feisty!

I think also of Deborah who was the only woman judge of Israel. It says clearly in the Book of Judges that Deborah was an authority figure in her time. People would come to her for judgement, for rulings, and for advice. She was also a military leader and led the Jewish people into battle, sort of a Joan of Arc. Deborah was clearly within the Jewish tradition.

In the Talmud there is a story about Bruriah who was so scholarly, it is said that she could learn three hundred laws in one day and often put the other students to shame. She is described in the Talmud as being so wise and so well-respected that she was as close to a woman rabbi in that period of history as we are ever going to get. Of course, unfortunately the male rabbis of the Talmud were uncomfortable with Bruriah's power and her position in the community and there are ambiguous questions regarding her death. An apocryphal story is told that perhaps she killed herself after a terrible experience of being seduced by one of her husband's male students. It is a sad story because it shows us how very threatening it is when women achieve some level of authority.

New possibilities

What has been happening in the Jewish feminist community is very exciting because women are gaining a voice in all areas of Judaism. What worries me is that some may feel that we might need permis-sion to find and use that voice. We have permission! Permission is given to us, not by men or by any human being, but by being who we are, by being alive and being God's creatures. We need to understand that we have permission to proceed.

I am reminded of a wonderful story by the biblical commentator Sforno, who uses the image of a tree and he says: "There are two kinds of trees. There's a tree that stands up straight against the wind and when a big gust of wind comes, it refuses to bend. What is going to happen to that tree? Eventually a gust of wind strong enough is going to knock it over. But there is a reed in the water," he says, "and the reed bends with the wind. When the wind comes the reed does not fight it. It goes with the wind and becomes one with the wind." Many people wish that Jewish feminists were just a little breeze. (It's just a few crazy women out there in the fringe who want to change everything!) No. I think we are the gust of wind and Judaism is either going to be the tree that will stand against us until it falls, or it will be like the reed in the water and bend with the changes and ultimately grow, blossom, and become more beau-tiful as a result. That for me is the crux of it, the challenge for Judaism. Will you take feminism seriously and bend with the wind, or hope that it goes away. It won't.

What Jewish feminists are presenting is truly universal for women of all religions. Women in the Catholic church, for example, are trying to get ordained as priests. Protestant women are dealing with the issue of the male personage and the male image of Jesus. Many of us have met. In Toronto there was a group called the Women of Faith — women clergy of all religions who would meet together and discuss issues. In Boston, where I lived, we had a group that meets over breakfast once a month to study issues of women in religion. The group is comprised of Catholic, Protestant, and Jewish women — Conservative and Reform. All of us are saying the same thing. Where is there room for us in our religion and what can we bring, as leaders and women, into our religious communities?

❧ Norma Baumel Joseph teaches in the Department of Religion at Concordia University, Montreal. In 1988–91 she was Scholar-in-Residence, at Montreal's Women's Federation of Allied Jewish Community Services. She founded, and is still involved, in a women's prayer group in Montreal and is founding member of the International Committee of Women at the Kotel.

NORMA BAUMEL JOSEPH

Though I feel very much part of the Jewish community, there are many ways I've been made to feel marginal, an outsider. By feminists, I am perceived as being too religious and too Jewish; by Jews, I am seen as too feminist. Some Jews see me as too Orthodox, others see me as not Orthodox enough.

Many people in the Jewish community are intimidated by my feminism. One rabbi in Toronto felt so threatened by me that he called me a "Jezebel." Jezebel was a Biblical queen who led the Israelites along the path to idolatry. She was a danger and a threat. When the rabbi called me that name, at first, I was terribly hurt. I wanted to bring Judaism to the world, not destroy it. I was not an idol worshipper, or in any way a sexual temptress, or any of the images he thought were evoked by calling me a Jezebel. I knew he was wrong, but since I had no forum for justifying myself, I simply continued teaching. In the end, there were two interesting consequences as a result of the whole experience. First, when I went to Israel, I was welcomed among the Israeli feminists, who had read about the Jezebel incident and decided that I must be "O.K." because of it. The second result was that I decided to include Jezebel in my repertoire of Biblical women. There are many interesting figures in the Bible and I want to celebrate many of them on different levels. I now dress up as Jezebel on the holiday of Purim.

A story of self-inclusion

As a little girl I remember enveloping myself in my father's prayer shawl, when I was still allowed to sit with him in the men's section of the synagogue, and liking the feeling. Praying in the synagogue I noticed the men wrapping themselves in their *tallitot* (prayer shawls) and it became more and more an intriguing part of my life. I began to speculate on what it would be like to be wrapped in a *tallit*, but I resigned myself to the fact that girls did not wear prayer shawls.

After I was married, I did not dwell on it but still I enjoyed seeing the men wrapped in their *tallitot*, and I wanted to be wrapped in something sacred to help me in my prayer. Finally, one day I talked to my husband, who is a rabbi, about it. We studied together and found that the permission for women to wear a *tallit* was to be found in some of the ancient sources. I really could wear one.

When my husband returned from a trip to Israel, he brought me a *tallit* as a gift. Though he urged me to wear it in the synagogue, I was reticent. I was afraid to upset the congregation and I was afraid of the responsibility that went along with wearing a *tallit*. I did not set out to be a rebel. I only wanted to do what was right halachically and right for me. I had to find my own way.

Finally, my husband said, "Nu, already? I bought you a gift; use it!" I tried it on and it felt right, it felt good. Wrapped in the *tallit*, I felt attached to God. In fact, the fringes on the prayer shawl are symbolic of attachments to God and God's law.

As it turned out, when I started wearing it to the synagogue I was pregnant. The congregation thought that I must be wearing it because there was something wrong with the baby and some rebbe recommended wearing a *tallit* to protect the unborn child. My husband and I tried to explain that I was perfectly healthy and wore the *tallit* out of religious motivation. Still, many members persisted in their superstitions. When the baby was born and I continued to wear the *tallit* some people said to me, "Oh, what a cute shawl; it looks like a *tallit*," to which I would respond, "It doesn't look like one; it is one!" After a time, although no other women wore a *tallit* mine was finally accepted in our congregation.

Not long after, my husband and I invited a young, out-of-town couple to come to our synagogue and then to join us for lunch. I knew the woman wore a *tallit*, and when she came into the synagogue she put it on. We simply nodded to each other in greeting and continued to follow the prayer service. After the service was over, I noticed a large group of women surrounding her and I felt pleased that our congregation was welcoming a stranger in their midst. When she was alone, I went to greet her and said, "Well, isn't it nice how they welcomed you." Her quick response was, "Welcomed me?" and she related how the female congregation members had told her about the terrible things that would happen if she wore a *tallit*: she risked becoming sterile; she would be barren. I was dumfounded. My friend continued, "I even said to them, what are you talking about? Your rabbi's wife, your own rebbitsen wears a *tallit*!" Then the women all said, "Oh, her? She's crazy!"

Feminism revitalizing Judaism

When I first began my journey as feminist and a Jew, I did not know where it would lead me. I wondered if there was going to be a clash between being female and being Jewish. Where I felt uncomfortable about certain things, I felt more strongly about the need to find out about them. Even though I had a good Jewish education, even though I had been raised in a very traditional household that believed in educating its daughters, I still felt ignorant. Every time I came to a moment of discomfort, of questioning, for example, who could wear a *tallit*, it meant going back to study. Feminism motivated me to learn text. It made me read the Bible and learn Talmud and now I was learning with adult perceptions. It invigorated my Judaism because I saw that Judaism could survive. I was optimistic that this flexible system called Judaism would meet any challenge and it would continue. On occasion it has been a painful journey but the two parts of me — Jew and female — are whole, integrated, and real. That is an incredibly liberating feeling. So, more and more I kept working towards it through study and ritual.

I thought about my obligations as a Jew and a female. For example, I wanted to pray publicly every day and I questioned why only males pray every day. I found out that women are obligated to pray daily, also. This real, ceremonial and religious reaction came about because I had to ask the feminist question first. In terms of study and teaching, feminism has pushed me and invigorated my Judaism. Feminism also makes me think about Judaism in very personal and very real terms.

I see the text as sacred because it emanates out of God and out of Jewish community; God empowered the community to create the text as it developed. I challenge the text because I am part of the Jewish community; for thousands of years, Jews have been trying to understand the text and attempts to understand has led to interpretation of it. Every generation has done that. Our Jewish libraries are filled with volumes of various interpretations. I don't challenge the text to defeat it. I challenge the text to bring it to life for me and my generation.

There can be important differences between the actual text and its popular interpretation. The Bible and the Talmud were sometimes taught to me in ways that made me feel like a second-class citizen, or certainly less than Jewish males. So in my journey of study, I focused on the text, first Bible and then Talmud. My questions were about the exclusion which came through the teachings, where it came from and what it meant.

One glaring misinterpretation of text is the phrase *"ezer k'negdo"* in Genesis 2:20. Commonly, it is interpreted as "a helper fit for him," Adam, or a "helpmate." Many interpreters treat the creation of Eve as being "less than," less important than or less than equal to the creation of Adam. Through this interpretation, Eve is seen as being created to serve Adam.

After studying the texts and Jewish commentaries on the text, I discovered that traditional interpretations did not add this aspect of subservience to Eve. Some commentators treated Eve as the creation of culminant perfection because God created life forms with a certain hierarchy, and Eve was the crown. All of the commentators treated the passage as two people created to walk side by side, two halves that form a complete pattern. If there is any skewing of control and dependence, the text later states, in Genesis 2:24, that the man must "cling to" and be dependent upon his wife.

In reading all these commentaries, I came across other comments which led to still more questions. For instance, Rashi states that a wife will help a good husband, but if her husband is not good, she will oppose him. So the whole issue of a woman promising to obey her husband in marriage is non-Judaic. In marriage, the partners are meant to stand on an equal plane. And since *ezer* is one characterization of God in the Bible, it seems unlikely that the interpretation of *ezer* should be as less than; it is possible that western values have coloured the interpretation because western society considers helpers less than, second-class.

A related instance of examining text and its interpretation is the passage where God tells Abraham "*shmah b'kolah,*" listen to Sarah's voice. Abraham at first does not want to take Sarah's advice, but after God's directive, he must. From that, I realized that women's voices are supposed to be heard, that the men in the community — husbands, sons, friends, rabbis — must hear us out. The *shmah b'kolah* does not imply that men should obey women in every case, become dependent in that sense. It means that the males should treat us women as the equals we are, both created in God's image. I, too, am part of the Jewish community and have something to give. I care, just as Sarah, a symbolic Jewish mother, cares about the Jewish people.

Understanding this text made me realize that I did not have to stay silent. I am a Jew and a human being created in God's image. This affirmed for me the right to speak out and not have my motives misunderstood as rebelliousness or misplaced anger. I love Judaism; I love being a Jew. I want the community to survive and the tradition of Judaism to continue into the future. I want to have a part in making that future and I won't be silent.

My favourite example of Judaism's ability to meet challenges to change and remain Judaism is the issue of women as formal students of Jewish texts. There always had been women in Jewish history who had studied and become learned. They were determined individuals but did not represent the norm. At the turn of this century, Sarah Shenirer and others developed a strategy to get Jewish women studying, stressing the need to have an educated group of Jewish women rather than lose them to assimilation. The rabbis agreed, and the Beth Jacob school system was started. So now we have a notion that Jews must teach not just their sons, but teach their daughters as well. They must teach their daughters not at their mother's knee, but in a school where the girls have access to formal instruction in Jewish knowledge. Today, everybody believes that a primary principle of ancient Judaism is the education of one's daughters. We know it is relatively new, but it is Judaism.

Rabbi Moshe Feinstein was a famous orthodox leader who wrote seven volumes of responsa — detailed answers to questions, some having to do with women studying. In answer to the simple question "Can women study?," he doesn't answer, "Yes, they can because . . . ." It is assumed that women will study. Feinstein's concern is that women get a Jewish education. When he says, "fathers must pay for their daughters' education," it meant that daughters should not be relegated to the public school system while sons got Jewish educations. Daughters would be learning other people's customs, not Jewish customs, in this other world of public school. Feinstein likens this to having a daughter kidnapped, and since Jewish law is clear that a father is obligated to ransom his daughter from a kidnapper, Feinstein concludes that the parents are obligated to pay for the education of their daughters.

Examples such as these are brilliant, creative interpretations of Jewish law. It's not about writing new law; it's pulling the salient points out from the surface problem. So the question about daughters' schooling is not really about paying or not paying a fee to a school, it is about ransoming her mind.

The roles of Jewish women

Some people think the traditional role for a Jewish woman is to be in the home and not to be a public figure. Many Jewish people would agree with this, but as a historian, I would counter that it is only in the last two hundred years, maybe less, that the role of Jewish women has been in the private sphere. I looked back into history to discover the precedents for myself: to function in public, to stand out; not to be only in the home, but to go out, to teach, to work with women. I had to go back into history to see what our great grand- mothers were doing.

Beginning in the Bible, I found incredible images of women who spoke out, women who did not deny their home life but also did other things. The Bible tells us about Deborah as a leader of men and women, a victorious leader in battle, a poet who would sing out and dance. The Bible had no trouble with the vision that has been brought forward of women taking action. The Bible unapolo- getically shows Sarah telling Abraham what to do and Rivkah rather than Isaac deciding how and who should be his true heir. There were many other examples throughout history of women working alone, women with other women, women working with men and women, continuing the role of family and continuing a role in the community. From Rufina to Rebecca Tiktiner, from Donna Gracia Mendes to Licoricia of Winchester, from Havah Bachrach to Sara Copia Sullam, Jewish women participated in the life of the community.

96

It became apparent to me that there were numerous historical patterns that I could use to build a bridge between my past and my future. These patterns also reinforced my decision to function in the public sphere. I was examining the process of becoming a public person, continuing my home responsibilities, and maintaining my own sense of privacy.

I was compelled by a desire to teach and I love teaching. Above being a special experience for me, teaching fills my desire to communicate with women. Every time I discovered something new about being female and Jewish, I wanted to share that knowledge. I wanted to communicate what those discoveries might mean, so I had to find outlets in which to teach. Montreal affords me wonderful opportunities to teach different people in many varied environments: women's study groups, at university, at the community centre. I feel right in what I'm doing. The biblical and historical figures are riding with me. I feel that what I was doing and what I continue to do is constructive, both to Judaism and to the traditional role of Jewish women before me.

Another of Rabbi Feinstein's responses has to do with women as teachers. He asserts that women can teach — and can teach men and women — as long as they are knowledgeable, as long as they have studied sacred text. The original prohibition against a woman teaching a man was established because of the possibility of sexual impropriety if sexual segregation were not strictly observed. Feinstein knows that in North America, women teach men in the *yeshivot*, the religious Jewish schools. So he analyzed the original reason for prohibition and concludes that in the present context of groups of students in educational institutions, there is little chance of sexual transgressions. Here, Feinstein gives an old law new reality. He reinterprets the old legislation. It's interesting that at the end of his response, he maintains that he prefers women teaching women and men teaching men, but he does not let his preferences interfere with the principle of women being able to teach, of women being knowledgeable.

Creating feminist ritual

Rosh Chodesh is a new moon celebration. The Jewish calendar is based on the lunar cycle, so the waxing and waning of the moon fits into the Jewish prayer cycle. At one time, Rosh Chodesh was a popular local celebration, of relaxation and enjoyment. Unfortunately, it has gone into disuse. As Jewish women began searching for new possibilities of affirmation, of celebration, they rediscovered Rosh Chodesh. This had been uniquely and specifically a women's holiday, partly because of the link to women's monthly cycle that seemed to fit the lunar cycle, partly because the women of Israel were responsible for many acts of redemption in Egypt and later on in the building of the temple. There was a notion that women deserved a holiday once a month. So women would get together on Rosh Chodesh and celebrate together. When the modern feminist movement challenged us, we responded by reviving Rosh Chodesh as a good time for women to be together. Now there are a number of communities that celebrate prayer and/or study for women around the Rosh Chodesh cycle.

The Rosh Chodesh ritual is extremely important for me. It feeds my desire to publicly experience my Judaism in a ritual context. I had already learned that the Talmud allows women to have an *aliyah,* even if custom tries to forbid it. My husband suggested that I pray with women. Part of me still wants the ultimate, the full, shared participation in the congregation, but I realize that it would not have been a wise first step. The logical first step was to learn to have an *aliyah* and to do that in the supportive company of other women. In Montreal, we've formed a group of women who come together on Rosh Chodesh to pray. We pray using the traditional prayers of *shacharit*; we omit certain prayers. We have *aliyot*, and read the Torah, and study together. In the end, I've loved praying with women; it has a special poignancy.

What is interesting to me is that I was not always prepared for where the journey would lead. I began the Rosh Chodesh services because I wanted an *aliyah*, which was and remains important and meaningful. However, the most religiously moving part of the prayer service turned out to be when I take the Torah out of the Ark and sing out the accompanying prayer. I feel I am standing in the shoes of Jews doing what Jews have always done, proclaiming the Torah emanating from Zion. I am incredibly empowered as a Jew, and this has become the most precious moment of the prayer service for me.

Creating new stories

One way Jewish women today are trying to approach text is through writing of *midrashim*. Midrash is the scope of traditional stories about the heros and heroines and events in the Bible. The tradition of midrash, mostly anonymous stories, is one which legitimately attempts to explain all kinds of interesting questions that bothered Jews throughout different generations. *Midrashim* tries to fill in the gaps in the text. It took women a long time to learn that they could also be part of the story-telling process, create their own *midrashim*. Women are now looking at the stories and asking, "What do these stories mean to me, and where do the gaps leave room for me to find my own voice through Judaism?" So now there is the beginning of *midrashim* by women, for women, about women's experience, and these stories use the heros and heroines of Biblical stories. This new Midrash is not an attempt to destroy Judaism, but to continue the tradition of it.

An example of a new Midrash topic is the story of Jepthah's daughter. It is extracted from a story in the book of Judges about a man who led the Jews to military victory through battle. His daughter is unnamed, an anonymous woman who is a tragic figure. Jepthah makes a vow that if he is successful in war, he will sacrifice to God the first being that exits from his home upon his return. The first being that exits is his daughter. We find ourselves faced with a story about human sacrifice, and unlike the story of the near-sacrifice of Isaac, we are faced with a story that allows the tragedy to happen. The creators of early *midrashim* worried about this story, so they gave the daughter a name and dealt with some of the issues. To create a midrash today, I think women would pick up the story at the moment after she agrees to self-sacrifice. The midrash would begin when the daughter replies that she will do as he promised, but she would like to spend two months with her female friends in the mountains. I would want to deal with why she wanted to be with women and what occurred during those two months? What did they do? How did they celebrate life, their youth, and mourn the upcoming tragedy? The *midrash* could conclude with the fact that every year after the sacrifice of Jepthah's daughter, women continued to mark this event with a celebration. We could begin again to celebrate Jepthah's daughter and weave our *midrash* into this new ritual, which is really an old ritual revitalized, a new story that is about a woman and her tragedy and her female friends.

Toward a stronger community

I am often asked, and it bothers me, whether Jewish feminists are creating a new community that will be separate from the general community. Ultimately, my feminism tells me to find a place for women within Judaism, not to make a Judaism that is exclusively for women. I think that would be counter-productive, just turning the pyramid over. It would be reverse-scale misogyny, and I don't want that to happen. I want my feminism to say that women are Jews and men are Jews; I recognize and celebrate that.

There are times for Jews — men and women — to be together. We work together, go to lectures together, pray together in communities. There are also times when I need to be with my women friends only. As I indicated in discussion on Rosh Chodesh services, there are differences in being only with women. It's not that I want only to pray with women, but there are times when I want to pray only with women. And sometimes I want to be alone and other times I need to be with Jews. I think we need an egalitarian feminism in Judaism, a sharing between Jewish men and women. It is also necessary to separate out, either as individuals or along gender lines at times. These separations are not the problem. The problem is what these separations have come to symbolize and what avenues are available for integration.

The synagogue where I pray has a *mehitzah*, a separation that divides the men from the women in the congregation. In some ways it feels right because it symbolizes for me an ability to pray alone while being in congregation. What feels wrong is that the *mehitzah* has come to symbolize, for too many people, that women are adjunct, they don't have to pray or their praying is less valuable. The other wrong feeling is that of hiding women, ostracizing them because they are somehow polluted. In a few synagogues, there is a

101

mehitzah down the middle of the synagogue, so men and women have equal access, physically and symbolically. They can remain separate so there is no flirtation or distraction, and both the men and the women can concentrate. When I pray, I concentrate so hard. It is so difficult to face God that I would rather not expend any energy on controlling distractions. So I want a *mehitzah* because it helps me control distractions and because it separates me from my husband. I love my husband; I'm overcome by love of him. If I sit next to him, it's easier to feel comforted in his love than to face the challenge of loving God. I want a *mehitzah* there as an empowerment. The separation also encourages women to be recognized as a separate being, not only as "wife of," and it creates a place for single women to feel included, rather than alienated in a coupled world. And in all this, the autonomy the *mehitzah* creates makes it possible for women to pray alone, to stand alone on her own merits to try to meet God.

NORMA BAUMEL JOSEPH
Following my Own Path. A speech delivered in Jerusalem, December, 1988 at the International Jewish Feminist Conference.

I am a Jew. I am a believing and practicing Jew and I choose to be an Orthodox Jew. There is nothing about that reality that I wish to deny. I find meaning and promise, challenge and conflict in my existence as a female Jew. Frequently I feel divided as though parts of myself are in opposition — antithetical, contradictory, antago'nistic, clashing, hostile. I wish to live as part of a community but I am often alone, an outsider. In a culture that values separation, *Kedoshim Tih'yu*, the command to be holy also means 'separate yourself,' I am often too separate.

These feelings rushed in on me one Shabbat morning as I stood with Alice Shalvi at the back of the men's section in my synagogue in Montreal. We were waiting for the rabbi, my husband, to call Alice forward. She was about to address our congregation on the occasion of Israel's fortieth anniversary. I felt her tension and anxiety as she was about to speak from the pulpit of an Orthodox synagogue on the Sabbath morning for the very first time.

As she began, Alice uttered the traditional blessing, *she'hecheyanu*, for something truly new was happening. But what was new and why all the tension? Jewish women speaking in public places is not new though perhaps rare. Certainly Miriam, Deborah, and Huldah pose as clear prototypes for us. Women as teachers of the community are also not new, not unheard of, like Bruriah, Asnat Barzani, Miriam Shapira Luria, and today Nehama Leibowitz. Perhaps the combination of function and place, of giving a sermon from the pulpit is remarkable, yet I can name such women as Bat Halevi, Dulce of Worms, Eidele of Belz, and the most famous Hannah Rachel Werbemacher, the maid of Ludomir. So Alice standing in front of my congregation was not the first woman to do so, yet clearly the experience was exceptional. Examples of female scholarship, leadership, and participation from the past are neither well-known nor proclaimed as precedence for our current involvement. What was truly new about Alice speaking from the pulpit was the vision we had of Alice and women like her who would participate and lead in the formation, in the dynamism, and in the shaping of what Judaism and the Jewish community might become. It was a vision of the empowerment of Jewish women within the tradition that is the topic here.

Women taking the path of scholarship, empowering themselves through the road of study is probably one of the greatest innovations of twentieth century Judaism. Girls are now expected to attend Jewish schools. The assumption that girls are included in this "Jewish" value of study is new. Debbie Weisman has shown us just how revolutionary a model of women's education can be even as it emanates from the Beth Jacob movement. Today, the Beth Jacob school system is the most conservative in its approach. Women have entered "the world of our fathers" in their pursuit of Jewish knowledge so that we have women today teaching and studying the sacred texts. These are women who feel compelled to continue their studies beyond high school; women who sacrifice their leisure hours in order to "learn"; women who feel compelled to become learned.

I have decided to follow that particular path of empowerment, to take the Jewish tradition of learning seriously and to forget that the command to study, the idealization of the learned one, only meant the boys. It is not easy. In the world of *halachic* scholars, I am a novice — I have not had the years nor the opportunities. I am not a *yeshiva bocher*. Among many Jews, male and female, I am a usurper, a Jew out-of-place. For me this path has been very difficult involving learning a new language, a new idiomatic structure, a new way of thinking. It has also been difficult because so many misunderstand my motives and misrepresent what I am trying to do, but the new learning has been marvellous and I know that I bring something important and unique to the material.

I must also say that the road has been difficult in ways I never expected. I knew the *yeshiva* world would not like me. I even knew I would be too feminist for the Jewish world, but when the feminist world finds me too Jewish and the Jewish feminist world finds me too religious, I find it too difficult. Always an outsider. Women have tried to redirect me or disempower me as frequently as men and I reject that. I reject their patronizing concept of me as an Orthodox Jew. You do not know me because you can label me. You do not know my politics nor my radical feminism and you cannot tell me I am not there yet.

¶ *Naomi Goldenberg is professor of Psychology of Religion and Coordinator of Women's Studies at the University of Ottawa, and Co-chair, Women and Religion section of the American Academy of Religion. She is the author of three books including* Changing of the Gods *(Beacon Press) and her most recent* Returning Words to Flesh *(Beacon Press, 1990).*

NAOMI GOLDENBERG

I think that central elements of our major religious traditions are destructive for women. It is very important that we think about the kinds of attitudes we need to create to be able to change these destructive ideas. A number of groups in society, have been diminished by traditions in which the power to determine behaviour is decided by a small group of men. The oppression of women and the internalized self-hatred that results from centuries of being told by men what to be and what to think, has been very harmful.

In the West, women are just beginning to exercise some sense of self-worth and dignity. I think you can see this in all the wonderful cultural forms, such as women's literature, film, and art, that are flourishing because of a sense of independence from men that women are now experiencing. Oppression is not good for people. Clearly it is not good for women — half the world's population — and I don't think it is good for men either to have the experience of being reflected back at twice their normal size.

It seems to me that many men do not have a sense of the broader context in which women and children live. For example, most patriarchal religions separate men from the care of young children. They separate men from the day-to-day living and sustenance that is necessary to run a family. Few men have an idea of the kind of domestic labour that allows them to go to work. Many men have women as their, well, I would say, as their servants, who take care of the laundry, the food, daycare, etc. I think that these men need to have more of a sense of the total context of living. The reason I say this is because I see men's power as being out of control.

The men with power in the world have massive means of destruction at their disposal. Because of this, I think we need to place limits on the power men hold over groups, such as families, or territories, or nations. This is the second reason why I feel that our religious traditions are so destructive — because most of them are about possession. They are concerned with possession of a tribe, of a land, of a woman, of a child.

I think that because of the heightened capacity for destruction that actually is in the power of various men all over the world, there has to be a rethinking of tribalism and of loyalty to male religious figures or divinities. Religions such as Islam and Christianity teach loyalty to male figures, to Mohammed and Jesus. In Judaism, there is a sense of loyalty to the tribe of Moses, or to various tribes headed by men. So, the world is divided up into male teams, and women are following along behind them. These teams are getting out of control. The game is getting much too serious. It's getting much too destructive.

For this reason, we have to be more humble and we have to make sure that men are more humble. We have to reform our religious traditions, to rethink the concept of control over a population.and to develop more tolerance for diversity. I really don't think that patriarchal religious traditions, as they stand, can accomplish this.

Jewish identity

The birth of my daughter has made Judaism even more problematic for me because I have to search out ways to give her a sense of Jewishness. I checked out a Jewish day school in my area and I realized that if I sent her there I would be in a froth of anger for the whole time she attended. I looked in the library and found that they had rows and rows of biographies but they were all of Jewish men. There were three copies of the same biography of Golda Meir. Of course there were pictures of great Jews on the walls — all huge pictures of men. I realized I could not send my daughter there. I also did not want her to have to contend with the exclusion that the Jewish community imposes on children of mixed marriages, since her father is not Jewish. Therefore, I am going to have to find other ways to connect her to Jewishness. I have sent her to Jewish summer day camps and she has participated in Jewish groups. She does know she is Jewish and she talks about being both Canadian and Jewish. I am raising her as an atheist which I feel is a reputable Jewish position.

I want my daughter to have a Jewish identity because it is a source of strength for me and because I think it is a way of fighting against the dominant Christian ethos. It also will provide her with a chisel to chip at the sameness of the world. I see it as a way of fighting against the Christian ethos, which is so pervasive. However, I want her to learn that she is not solely a Jew; that we are all many things and have many identities.

I have always felt excluded from the Jewish community. I know

109

that this feeling resulted from being raised in a poor family in a very wealthy Jewish town in the United States. It was expensive to belong to the synagogues and that was the reason my parents gave for our not belonging. I always felt separate from other Jews and this gave me a sense of being on the outside looking in. The neighbour⁄hood where we lived was in the Christian part of town, which meant that I also felt excluded from the Christian community since I was being raised as a Jew in a kosher house.

Yet it is very important for me to affirm my Jewish identity and to feel connected to Judaism. For me, what is most valuable about being Jewish, is that it fosters scepticism. If you study the history of the Jewish people you can clearly see the horrible results of oppres⁄sion and hatred. You learn to think very carefully about power and the abuses of power and the terrible things that can happen when one group is perceived as being radically different from others. I think that the study of Jewish history should make Jews very sensitive to oppression in the world.

The world needs to be healed with the Jewish idea of *tikkun olam*. This concept is a very important part of my thinking. My Jewish⁄ness is part of my wanting things to be changed. I see Jewish thinkers such as Emma Goldman, Karl Marx, and Sigmund Freud as people concerned with freedom and with changing different struc⁄tures of oppression. I like what I see as a rebellious, disruptive quality in Jewish history. But I'm worried that this element of Judaism is diminishing, since there is now a practice of defining very closely what is Jewish, what isn't Jewish, and what belongs to Jews. My concern is with the defensiveness of the Jewish community. There seems to be too much justification for oppressing other people. I think it is a totally un⁄Jewish justification of imperialism, of sup⁄pression of other people's civil rights. I find that very distressing. If there's a lesson in the holocaust, if there's a lesson in Jewish history, it's that the oppression of any people is a terrible thing. In that sense, I feel myself as very Jewish, because I'm always uncomfortable with authority and with structures, and I'm always questioning people's right to control others. I'm uncomfortable when lines of authority get drawn too tightly in any place — in the university, in the classroom, in the State, and in intellectual discussions. This is a part of my Jewishness that I would like to see communicated to my daughter.

When I was twenty-one, I went to Israel right after the Six-day War. It was so exhilarating to be walking around Jerusalem. It was the first time in my life that I had been in a city where I felt that somehow my personality and my character were more typical than atypical. I loved it. I felt that I wanted to live in Israel.

But after hearing and reading about so many of the things that are happening in Israel now and which have been happening for a long time (even in the 1960s), I am disturbed. I am disturbed about the treatment of the Arabs and the Palestinians. It bothers me very much that Israel is not a wholly democratic state. I think that Jewishness as I define it, that incredible sense of justice and sensitivity to injustice, should be called upon to correct the injustices in Israel now.

I am encouraged by the forces in Israel, the groups who feel the way I do, and I give them my complete support. I think the feminist movement has an important role to play. As I see it, feminists question the tribal boundaries that men have set up. Why should we just be loyal to the Jewish people? I feel that the Palestinians are my people too. Why shouldn't we feel solidarity with them? My sense of oppression as a Jew binds me to people who have also been oppressed. I see the feminist movement in Israel as something very, very positive. I hope it will move in the direction of encouraging identification with many peoples.

111

It is important for Jews to understand that Judaism has many links with paganism. The adjective "pagan" simply describes a person who lives in the country. Paganism itself is the worship of nature. There are many divinities within paganism. There are divinities of streams and rocks and trees. Judaism has traditionally denigrated such beliefs as idol worship. But actually, when we think about it, we have to ask what's wrong with valuing a stream or a rock or a tree?

It is hard to know what the position of women actually was in pagan societies. In some cases, it seems to have been better than it was within traditional Judaism. In other cases, it seems to have been worse. This is a subject that needs a lot of study and attention. One thing that seems certain to me is that Judaism has more links with pagan practice than has been thought. In fact, Judaism rests on a stratum of paganism, as we can see if we examine the Jewish holidays. For example, Hannukah commemorates a military victory. But actually, the holiday was grafted on to the pagan celebration of the winter solstice. That's really why we light candles. They are linked to the anticipation of the return of the sun, to the time when the light begins to come back to the earth. Christianity also has a festival of light at this time — one which celebrates the birth of the sun child. Both Judaism and Christianity are grafted on to an older pagan religion — a religion that is connected with a sense of the earth and the movement of the planets.

The bar mitzvah is a ritual of adult male initiation into Judaism. It is a celebration welcoming a young man into his community. However, to fully understand this, we must ask what is happening to young girls of the same age. They are usually beginning menstruation and thus becoming adult women. The Jewish psychoanalyst

Bruno Bettelheim saw the bar mitzvah as a male imitation or appropriation of the initiation that women naturally undergo with menstruation. The male social event receives more emphasis than the female bodily event. Thus within Judaism there is both an appropriation of pagan practices and of female life cycle events.

I think the study of paganism and the effort to look at Jewish goddesses and their relationship to Canaanite figures in early Jewish history will help us loosen up Judaism. It will also help us to see other possibilities for rituals that could incorporate women more profoundly, rituals that are more ancient than those we practice now.

It may seem contradictory for me to be an atheist who thinks goddess religions are important. However, I see religious symbols as metaphors for thinking. Even if you do not believe in the male gods of your culture, you cannot help being affected by the sense of their importance. Whether you believe or not is actually irrelevant. Therefore, the presence of goddess imagery is important for women. It is not necessary that women believe in the existence of goddesses, but rather that symbols of goddesses be present to feed human imagination. We need to put more emphasis on female presence in the world. That is why I see goddess religion as valuable even though I am an atheist. Instead of believing in a god or a goddess, I believe in the power of symbols to evoke possibilities in people. I am affected by goddess imagery and I understand this effect as both psychological and metaphoric.

I believe in people. We are so complex that we need different symbols to express our varying experiences. Goddess imagery can evoke significant memories and feelings in both women and men. When you think about it, everyone's first relationship is with a woman. We all begin our lives within a female body and thus our earliest relationship with a woman is very intense. In a sense, we all begin life as women. If there is any value at all to Jung's idea of the anima in men, it lies in this reality that men are originally women. Most patriarchal religions are based on the rejection of womanliness in men. This seems to be why it is so crucial in Judaism for a man to thank God that he is not a woman. The famous prayer is one way for men to insist that they are grown up and thus grown away from needing or being like women.

Therefore, I see goddess religion as serving two purposes. It can both recall the maternal context in which we begin life and return us to the veneration of nature. Such awareness is necessary to help us counteract destructive power in the world. We need the kind of animation that is present within paganism and that I believe is still present within the ancient history of Judaism.

It's very important to me that Jewish scholarship be concerned with revealing the politics behind the Torah and the Talmud. I would like to make it clear that in no way do I consider these texts to be sacred or divinely inspired. I think they need to be analyzed with an eye to uncovering the social situations that both inspired them and emphasized some over others. One important dimension of the political context of all of the texts is that they were constructed in societies in which men dominated women.

We cannot keep hanging on to these male texts. We need to take them apart. We need to understand how they arose. If we read them only obediently, in the context of the Jewish rituals, then we will continue to perpetuate their male perspective. These texts were written by men. They were written by men who were cared for by anonymous women, and the texts reflect this.

We also need to find other texts. Historians are beginning to uncover stories in the diaries of women. We need to find such texts and we also need to write new texts. We need to acknowledge that

114

the traditional texts were humanly inspired. But this doesn't mean that we should just disown them. We must keep the old as part of our heritage, because they are part of who we are. The male texts will always be part of us, but we need to supplement them, we need to enlarge our rituals to include other dimensions, to include the thoughts of women whose experience differs from those shown in the traditional texts.

Change and continuity

I particularly enjoy teaching my Women and Religion course, in which I have a mix of ages in the room — older and younger women from various religious backgrounds. Usually people who very much want to stay within their traditions do not take my courses. Those who are beginning to question things tend to sign up.

One woman I remember vividly, told me that after several months of my class, the required readings and lectures had ruined Catholicism for her. She could not attend church any more without feeling angry. She wondered what I was offering as an alternative. I realized that I had nothing to offer but the questions I asked. For me, the questions themselves are vital. Staid answers do not make me comfortable. I told her that I hoped in the future there would be answers and perhaps other forms of communities.

As yet there aren't many alternative communities. It seems that the only way for people to feel the warmth and security and sense of tradition they seek is still within the patriarchal religious traditions. Many people, including women, are returning to the patriarchal religions precisely because they offer a secure, familiar environment. However, I think this is destructive. I understand the need for patriarchal religion, but I think it more important that we learn to build alternative traditions — ones that are not defined along male tribal lines. I hope that alternative communities will develop so that I will one day be able to provide examples to future students.

I believe that women cannot feel valuable, dignified, or independent if they are subjected to religions with male gods like Jesus Christ, Allah, and Yahweh. If religions have primarily male figures such as Moses, Buddha, and Mohammed, and continue to focus only on men, then women will never be able to have a sense of their own dignity and value. The image of the divinities needs to be changed to include women. When I try to imagine women as rabbis, priests, and ministers, I realize that women in the clergy can't represent a male god — can't stand in for a male figure. Women ministers, rabbis, and priests need to change the texts and the gods to reflect images that are more like themselves, more feminine. In a sense, Pope Paul VI was right when he said that women priests can not represent a male Jesus Christ. I agree with him wholeheartedly about that. We need to have female imagery for the divine.

I think that women will be practicing something very different when they have a central place within Judaism. I see that as a healthy challenge. However, Judaism will have to change so much that I wonder whether it could remain the same religion. When I said this in my book, *Changing of the Gods*, some conservatives were very happy. They took it as an admission that feminist reform would mean the end of Judaism, and that therefore all feminists should be ignored. I do not think that is true. In a sense, Judaism can be whatever Jews decide it should be. I believe Judaism is what Jews do, therefore Jewish feminists can change it. By saying it would be something different, I want to underline the immensity of the change that I believe is necessary.

Putting women in the centre of the decision-making process

would certainly mean the end of a god who is exclusively male. I don't know whether this change would mean the end of each and every concept of god. I hope it would because I think it is very important to put the emphasis on people instead of on any god. The idea of a god up there, perhaps moving people like puppets or trying to do his best as a sort of tired bureaucrat, seems dangerous to me. We cannot delude ourselves this way. I want people to understand that the world is constructed by human beings, who make their own history, philosophy, and their own gods and goddesses. A feminist revolution would thus hopefully mean the end of god as we know him. I hope it would mean the end of beliefs in transcendent forces directing human life.

I thank Gillian Smith for her collaboration and careful editing of my spoken text — N.G.

DIALOGUE

❧ *This conversation between Norma Joseph and Naomi Goldenberg took place in Montreal, November, 1988.*

Norma Joseph & Naomi Goldenberg

Naomi:

I remember the first time I heard you speak. You spoke so powerfully and eloquently, even with a wonderful touch of anger in your voice, about including women in Judaism. During the question period, I asked how you could expect to include women in rituals, prayer, and in all aspects of Jewish life, when the texts had been authored by men, the rituals created by men, and when even the history consisted of men recording themselves over thousands of years.

You responded by saying that women were present throughout history and there was no way you were going to believe that women did not participate in those events and in those texts. You said that your work was to uncover that participation. It was an impressive answer but I didn't totally agree with you. I am still not prepared to accept the argument completely.

Norma:

And I've learned from you to be sceptical, so now we have both sides. I still say women were there. They participated and they practiced. If they were not always creating, they were involved in

118

creating. You cannot say, in order to make a feminist Judaism, I am going to write out the women who were part of the system. They were part of the system and their history is precious to me. The rituals that were done then were relevant to them. I want to keep that, but I also need to invigorate it with my own needs, my own voice, and my own presence. I also want to do the research to uncover when they did speak out clearly. Women are working in specific areas of study now. Chava Weissler has been concentrating on women's prayers. We now know that in the mediaeval era, women wrote and recited special prayers, *tehinot*. So I want to sing them. I don't want to forget the prayers that women have been saying, even though some of them were male-created, because women did say them. I don't want to wipe it out because men are still part of my community and I am not going to erase them either. Their creative energy and their parts still stand. I just need to add and be creative in the new synthesis that is going to come out of it.

Naomi:
It is very hard, I think, for men to give up their central location in the texts and in the prayers. This is what we feminists are talking about — a displacement of men. We have to be honest about that. In Judaism, men are accustomed to being the centre of everything, while women assist them. I don't see men's motivation for change. After all, they will have to take over some of the work women have done, like koshering the stove for the holidays and preparing some of the food. They will have to do these things to enable women to study. I think that it is going to be quite difficult for men.

Norma:
It is going to be difficult in two ways. First of all, it is equally as hard to convince women they can legitimately take centre stage as much

as it is to convince men to move aside a bit. Secondly, our image of what happened in the past is not necessarily accurate. For example, stories of my own grandfather being a great rebbe abound. We know of his publications and his work, and his own children worship him and only talk about him as a rabbi-scholar. But my mother told me that in the middle of the night when one of the children cried, he would pick them up, diaper them, calm them and place them in bed with my grandmother for nursing. My grandmother, who stayed asleep, would nurse the baby and then my grandfather would return the baby to its crib. We have in our own history, then, the role of men and women sharing much more than a 1950s imagery allows us. We have to go back further to find those images and take them into the future with us.

Naomi:
When I talk about change in Judaism, what I want is more flexibility, and I don't see that happening. I am looking for an accommodating Jewish community — for example, a community that would accommodate me. I am married to a non-Jew and I have never had a formal Jewish education. It is difficult to find a community for me and my family, and I have almost given up trying. If it weren't for the growing Jewish feminist movement, I might have given up already.

Norma:
But you haven't given up trying?

Naomi:
It seems to be even getting worse. Jewish communities are building up walls and defining themselves more narrowly. Perhaps they feel the nature of Judaism is being threatened. There are many people

in Israel who feel that they must have a strict definition of who a Jew is to keep certain people out and other people in control of defining things. It affects people like me who have always been on the fringe of the Jewish community. We become increasingly disaffected. It may be our loss but I think it is Judaism's loss as well.

Norma:
I think you are right. There is a growing inflexibility in Jewish communities which some call a movement to the right.

Naomi:
To be fair there is a growing inflexibility in most religious traditions. Fundamentalism is spreading all over the world. . . .

Norma:
. . . cross-culturally and it worries me because the brand of open Judaism that my husband and I practice is less and less prevalent. As much as I know that you yourself feel on the margins, I am very much there, too. Within the feminist community I am too Jewish and within the Jewish community, I am too feminist. It is in Jewish law and history where I begin to find the seeds for hope because in the legal system there is great flexibility. There is no statement that says no abortion. Instead, the law instructs us to look at the condition of the woman: what does she need? We can build flexibility into that kind of precedent. Every time I look at a Jewish legal answer, I see incredible adaptability. But I worry about the community's inability to bend. Their fearfulness seems to be pushing them to extremes that are not necessitated by the Judaic system, neither thought nor of law. That is why you have to transform the system from within. If we all give up, Judaism will move in an unwanted direction, and will no longer be recognizable as Judaism. I believe

121

my task is to stay and battle from within the community.

Naomi:
I am sure that your task is to work from the inside, but I think that people can work for change from different positions: inside, outside, or on the margins. For me, the essence of Judaism is a sense of justice and a sense of outrage at injustice in the world. This sense is not focused only on the Jewish people. Jews in Canada should have a lot of sympathy and express support for the Japanese-Canadians, and . . .

Norma:
The Inuit.

Naomi:
Yes, the Inuit. Our oppression as a group throughout history should make us more compassionate and aware of the oppression of other groups. To me, that is the fine stuff in Judaism — the sense of justice, the concern for careful analysis of issues, constant debate, scepticism. I find that to be the valuable core of my Jewish being, and that is what I want to see preserved.

Norma:
I don't see that you can preserve an intellectual tradition unless you also preserve the rituals and ceremonies with in. From my back-ground in anthropology, I have seen that cultures must stay together. Certain things change; there is diffusion, borrowing, and syncre-tism, but you cannot keep a cultural system all in your head. You cannot maintain values, ethics, and principles without enacting them in some way.

Naomi:

Oh, but the expression of principles may change. For instance, psychoanalysis is a Jewish creation. It originates out of a Jewish suspicion of the way things are and I think it is a great gift to the intellectual world. I see it as an outgrowth of Jewish thought.

Norma:

Yes, but let me give you an example of Passover. On Passover, we go through this incredible ritual, which means an enormous amount of work for me. Then, we sit down around the table and we talk about freedom and about exactly what you said. Know the oppressed because you were once oppressed. Reject slavery because you were once slaves. Celebrate freedom because you were once not free. Those are clearly the principles, but then Judaism says you cannot celebrate the principles and enact them in your life unless you ceremonialize or ritualize them. So you have to eat *matzoh*, the unleavened bread, and you have to drink the four cups of wine. And you must be happy. Then you go wash the dishes. It is an integrated thing. You have to be totally embodied in the moment and experience, and we will carry through the principles. But we need both the ritual and the principles.

Naomi:

There are some people who talk about "Judaisms" and about several beginnings for Judaism that involved female divinities and goddesses. I find their work fascinating because it opens up the possibility that many of the constructs for divinity that we have now in Judaism were formed in reaction to certain kinds of female deities. For example, there were female spirits who were worshipped under every tree and near every brook and stone. We need more of such goddesses, more of a sense of that kind of sacredness within Judaism.

It has been lost under the guise of a male monotheism. I know that some people see female aspects within Judaism's male god, but this is not enough for me. I think we need to recapture a sense of plurality and animation about many things in the world. Perhaps talking about polytheism may be one way to encourage this.

Norma:

That's the end of the line for me in that I'm a strict monotheist. I think Judaism can only be monotheistic and it has proclaimed itself so. I don't see any way of detaching the two.

On the other hand, if we talk about interpretation and about understanding theology, then we can begin to talk about the concept of God that has infinite sources within it. Once you say "infinite," it means that I can view God as my mother, as Shekhinah, imminent. All the aspects that a polytheistic system might have envisioned separately, I can see in holistic terms as different sparks of the one God, as the mystics do, or part of the infinite variety of godliness. So I can say that I pray to God in female imagery and still believe that I am a monotheist and that it is the God of my people and my ancestors. It is the God that appeared both to Abraham and to Sarah and it is the God I love. I can call that God she and he. I have found sources for that. When Judaism began, it was against idol worship, not female idol worship. It was against polytheism of all sorts. It was an attempt to say that there is one supernatural power with an infinite variety of terms of reference. So the Bible is fighting against the polytheism that you are interested in but it is open to pluralistic monotheism.

Naomi:

I can see your point there and I can see how you can make polytheism into monotheism that way. It almost becomes a question of

124

semantics. However, I feel that any monotheism that proclaims itself as being a single force, a single divinity, is perhaps fascistic. We have so much competition for power in the world now. I think the belief in monotheism and in only one way of regulating behaviour has become too dangerous. I would rather not play with the semantics of monotheism but simply say that there are many ways to be alive in this world and there are many patterns that are good. I am afraid that by maintaining monotheism, we are just feeding the ideal of 'mono' behaviour which is so troublesome in our world. Everyone is being subjected to a uniform standard — largely technological, North American, and Christian. While I know that much of Judaism stands against this, I feel that any monotheism proposes a standardization of human experience.

Norma:
I see it the opposite way. My monotheism is liberating me because it says there is a very big difference between unity and uniformity. Maybe we should call it infinitetheism instead of monotheism. Maybe there are problems with the word. But everything about God cannot be known. The Bible is very clear about that. Nobody can see God, nobody can know God. Seeing is knowing, so nobody can see God and live. But everybody — every tradition and culture — sees a little bit of God. In their own way, everybody experiences a small portion.

I can't say my way is better than yours, and that you have to change your ways because I know better. No. My way is for me, your way is for you, and we have equal respect. I must respect yours because you are part of this world that God created. The 'oneness' does not mean that you have to practice as I do. It means I am obligated to respect your way because you have seen another vision of God.

Naomi:
But what if I don't have any vision of god? And I don't. I am an atheist and I think that atheists can have a fine moral vision, because we are 'peoplists.' I am suspicious of any kind of theism that says there is a force in the world that sees everything but is itself unseen. I don't like the idea that you and I are only valuable to the extent that we personify a transcendent force. I want to put more emphasis on people. You are valuable to me because you are Norma, not because you represent some god who I cannot see but who sup-posedly sees everything. I think that within Jewish thought, there is a fine tradition of atheism and scepticism that is important to me. Sigmund Freud and Melanie Klein are two examples of great Jewish atheists whose work I value.

Norma:
But I believe in one God. Monotheism means that the people principle that I believe in is anchored in timeless, healthy truths. So the concept is even more elevated for me. It says the principles of egalitarianism, of humanity, of peopleness, of respecting you, are so much more than 'it feels right' to me. It's not just my subjectivity. It is the way the world can be. It makes me optimistic. I could look at people, especially given the events of this century, and become pessimistic and nihilistic. But instead of saying people are bad, evil, greedy in the worst sense, I want to focus on their capability to do good. I can say the good is part of what I believe God is all about.

Naomi:
So that God is basically good.

Norma:
God introduces the principles or the concepts of goodness in the

126

world and gives us choices. Choose life or choose death. There is good and there is evil and now it is up to you. People, go to work; here is a world I have created for you. There are infinite possibilities for you within that world; go do it the best you can.

Naomi:
It seems to me that such a god is being sadistic. If god has all the power to create a world such as the one you describe, then surely he can foresee the earthquakes and other devastating things that happen. If god lets these tragedies occur, then he can not be very good to begin with. That's an old argument. Furthermore, if god isn't good, why do I need him? If god can't do anything much about the bad in the world, then he is just like any other bureaucrat trying to do his best but failing miserably a good deal of the time.

Norma:
She is not like that.

Naomi:
Changing the gender of this god would not make a difference. Anytime I start thinking about what "god" is supposed to be, it seems to me a ridiculous belief. If I believe in people and I believe in the good and bad possibilities in people, I think I am on much firmer ground. I value people because it is they who determine my survival. We have to see that it is we who make up the world.

Norma:
Yes, and I think that is God's mandate to us. I could say the same thing. Why would God want to create people if everything was going to be simple and easy? You asked why have a God if things are going to be hard, and I would say why have people if things are

going to be easy. God created this order out of chaos with disorder in it so that we could create our own world. In other words, God made us creative beings.

Naomi:
But then he created us for his own amusement.

Norma:
She.

Naomi:
She created us for her own amusement.

Norma:
No. She created us to be independent: thinking, creating, beings with the choices of mature adults. We have the choice to do good and live in this world or to make mistakes and suffer the conse-quences. I don't believe we can sit back and say that God made me do it. That is not the answer. God didn't make us do Hitler or give in to Hitler. Human beings allowed it. We participated in it. We were part of it.

Naomi:
For me, a belief in god only cloaks over our human responsibilities. It hampers our understanding of human motives.

I don't think we can guarantee that the Judaism that exists now is going to continue if we make the changes that I think are necessary. I don't think we have to, or should, cling to Judaism as we know it. The religion is going to change and maybe it will change in some good ways that we can't even imagine now. I think it is wrong to hold on to something simply because of the fear of what change might bring. I don't want to keep tradition simply for its own sake. I don't think narrowly preserving the religion can yield the kind of equality, freedom, and justice that is, for me, Judaism's essence.

Norma:
I agree. I think we have to not cling to tradition out of fear but we can embrace some of the traditions out of love while at the same time interpreting and adding new possibilities and knowing that there are many Judaisms. The Judaism of the future won't be exactly what it is today, just as the Judaism of the past is not the same as present-day Judaism. The process of change has been good, and there is continuity. While we are creating the new, we can bring some of the traditions along with us. It is important not to destroy things simply because you want something new. If following the ideals of justice and freedom leads to . . .

Naomi:
. . . if it leads to new forms, well, then fine with me. And if those forms are Jewish or a combination of Jewish and something else, that is fine with me too.

Norma:
An important Jewish concept is fence-building as a protective measure. If you have a central law that you want to protect, you build a metaphoric fence around it, maybe two fences. What we've accomplished in the name of keeping tradition is to build so many fences that the central concept, Judaism, is in danger of caving in from the added weight. We can't let that happen. We have to go as far as we can, keeping the priorities and principles clear, but not overdo it, not stand so far back because of all the fences we've built that we lose sight of the centre.

Naomi:

Perhaps what is behind the fence will change and perhaps that won't be so bad. It is the tendency to build a fence to keep some people out and some people in that really bothers me about the direction that so much of Judaism is going in right now.

TRIALOGUE

❡ *This discussion took place in Toronto, May, 1988*

Naomi Goldenberg, Norma Joseph, Elyse Goldstein

Naomi:

I think the Bible is important for all people, all feminists, whether they believe in it or not, whether they are religious or secular. It is important for me as an atheist because it is a foundation for my culture. Yet, precisely because it forms so much of the basis of our thinking, we must take it apart and analyze it. We must know as much about it as we possibly can and that is why I strongly support the work that biblical scholars are doing. However, I don't think we should cling to the Bible as a model for living. It should not be considered our only foundational text. When Elizabeth Cady Stanton was working on *The Woman's Bible*, she said that we should treat the Bible as we would any other book. We must analyze the text, so that we can accept the positive things in it and be able to reject what we find to be negative.

Elyse:

I think what you are saying is challenging and kind of frightening to Jews who look at the Bible as the sacred literature. I have strong feelings about the way we might deconstruct it — after we are done taking it apart, do we put it back together again and put it on the table and say, "This is a nice book. We've approached it like we would Shakespeare and other great literature and they will all go very nicely on our shelf." As a Jew my Bible has a much bigger place for me than, for example, Shakespeare might have. Although I enjoy dissecting Shakespeare, I don't dissect it with the same reverence as I would the Bible. I study the Bible lovingly, caressing it, understanding it with my heart as well as with my head. I would think it is much more important to me than just great literature.

Naomi:
The Bible is more important because it has been treated as authoritative. However, it is parallel to great literature because specific human beings created it to reflect their own lives. Since their text is authoritative in my world, I should try to understand the politics of the people who wrote it.

Norma:
Yes, because it provides role models for us in certain ways. I am careful to dissect the Bible lovingly. I see all the layers of human creation in the text as well as in the history of interpretation of that text. The Bible is very important to our western culture, very foundational, but the traditions of interpretation are very different. On one level, we have one task: to understand the text as it stands. But then there's another process we have to go through, that is, how did the different traditions interpret the text? All those layers of interpretation are used in reading the text. It's difficult, but it's liberating. If I read the text one way and others have read it differently, I'm setting myself up against them. I'll have trouble claiming authority and legitimacy for my own interpretation of the text. But if I can point to Sforno and Ibn Ezra and Rashi, and list the generations of mediaevalists and modernists who interpreted the

same text differently, then I have some basis for argument.

Elyse:

What do you do when you see a text that clearly hurts you as a woman — let's say a text on women as property — and you look at the commentaries, at Ibn Ezra, Sforno, and Rashi, and they are either silent on the issue or their commentary further hurts you because it is so sexist? What if you are looking for an interpretation that values you as a woman and you just can't find it?

Norma:

That's my point. You have to be very careful when claiming the Bible as sacred because nobody claims all of the Bible as sacred. Nobody, in the most androcentric perspective of Judaism claims that we should be like Solomon and have one thousand wives. Nobody wants to follow certain models of Biblical patterning. Even those who use the term archetypal patterns to describe Bible don't want to claim all of it. Everybody selects segments and uses inter- pretation to get to certain segments.

You have to find yourself within your own tradition. First, I want to know what the text says. Then I want to know what Jewish interpretations have said and how diverse they've been. How con- frontational have they been, and has that been kosher? Then I can build on those layers, and where there are essences and segments of interpretations that resonate in my life, I will build on them, because it's authoritative. When there's text and interpretation that is prob- lematic, I must claim it. One story is that of Jepthah's daughter, who was sacrificed. As Jews, we love to proclaim the Bible, that Abraham was told not to sacrifice his son, Isaac. When Jepthah sacrifices his daughter, who remains unnamed in the text, nobody proclaims that. So I must proclaim it, as a segment of text that wounds me and sacrifices me today. Therefore, I don't want to wipe out that text; I must maintain its integrity, but I must also say, "That part can't be the desire of God. The word of God is that you must seek justice." The word of God had somehow been diverted, lost in that story. The story still must be told, but told with the interpretation and understanding that an event such as the sacrifice of Jepthah's daughter can no longer occur today.

Elyse:
We have to be honest when, we as feminists, do interpretation. Are we really uncovering the actual story or are we rewriting the story in our own image? Do we want so badly for the Bible to be feminist that we twist it around, that we undress it, and redress it to look feminist? When we peel off all the feminist clothing that we have put on, do we find out that it is truly sexist at its core and there is nothing we can do about it? No matter how we try and rewrite it, as feminists, the sexism stares us in the face still.

Norma:
No, what I am saying is two things. First of all, we have to declare, pronounce, and acknowledge the sexist elements. That's the story of Jepthah. You have to be aware that those elements do exist in sacred text, in the layers of interpretation. At the same time, we must legitimize our ability to write and interpret Midrash, just as Sforno and Ramban interpreted Midrash. Their commentaries are still maintained within the core of Judaism, with diversity, confrontation, and disagreement. These scholars followed some lines of continuity but also followed some lines of argumentation and disputation as well. I can identify problems in certain stories, and I have the ability to identify certain weaknesses in translations and improve upon their interpretation.

Elyse:
But Norma, why do you need male commentators to give you that permission.

Norma:
The male commentators did not give me the permission to under-stand the text. They are part of a Jewish community that I am part of, and they indicate that we have been interpreting text all along, as a community. The community has now defined itself as inter-preters and I am continuing that tradition. I am saying, "Let me in. I am a feminist but I am a Jew and my cry is that you count me not as equal to a man but as a Jew." That's my cry of feminism. I want to be a Jew, not a female Jew, a Jew. And as a member of the Jewish community, I can interpret. I don't think we want to apologize for text nor dress it up, but to do a feminist critique of text is what's exciting.

Naomi:
I think we have to do more than hold on to that particular text, going over and over it. I agree that we have to continue the tradition of interpretation but we also have to put the Bible in its own context. We have to look at how various texts were selected for inclusion in the Bible and how they also reflect the image of the men who wrote and chose them. If we stick to texts that men set up, we are going to be limited in what we do. For example, I think we have to look at the way the Jewish worship of goddesses might have been sup-pressed and also at the influence of the pagan traditions surrounding Jewish authors and communities. I don't think we should continue to hold on to the texts as if they were so vitally essential.

Elyse:
But we have to be careful because what scares me here is the common anti-Semitic notion that everyone worshipped goddesses until those Hebrews came along with their male God . . . .

Naomi:
No, no.

Elyse:
. . . and that's the end of the goddesses. Oh, those Hebrews!

Norma:
There is an anti-female and anti-Jewish sentiment in those kinds of statements.

My vision of a community that incorporates the feminist critique is a vision in which women are central, in which women are normative and their experiences are part and parcel of that dynamic. That is creative Judaism. No Judaism is monolithic or stationary. My hope for the future is that we claim our part on centre stage; not behind the scene nor on the side of the scene, nor passive, but active and central, and that becomes normative Judaism. Then no rabbi would be able to say, "All you Jews, all you Jews who are circum-cised," and not say, "Oh my goodness, I'm forgetting Jews who are female!" I have been in too many congregations where rabbis exclude me and that exclusion goes against the grain of my being a Jew. I have the ability to stand up and say, "I am a Jew. I am a participant in this Jewish community. I am equally entitled to the responsibilities of Judaism." I see a need for a critique in terms of Jewish feminist theology, of participation in ritual, and language modifications, as well as legal changes. I would also like to see a world in which the prayer books, the experiences, and the rituals all echo my own reality as a Jew who is female.

Elyse:
I remember reading an article in a Jewish newspaper a couple of years ago about Simchat Torah, the holiday celebrating the Torah. On Simchat Torah, it said, it is a Jewish custom to honour all the Jews of the synagogue with an *aliyah* (being called to read from the Torah). I read that line and I wondered which Jews he was talking about! To honour all the Jews meant all the male Jews. My vision for the community includes a female leadership because it would be impossible for a woman rabbi to think of 'all Jews' being only male. It is essential to have female leadership, with female biblical scholars, commentators and rabbis addressing the whole Jewish community.

Naomi:
Addressing the whole Jewish community but also addressing and learning from each other.

Norma:
And learning with women.

Naomi:
Yes, and learning from women. In the last several years, my contact with Jewish feminists has brought me more within Judaism and within debates about text and ritual. It has brought me closer to the Judaism that I have been away from for a long time — a Judaism I could never have experienced with men. I think we women have a lot of learning to do together.

Elyse:
It is very tempting to just separate and say, "I'm going to find a

community of feminist Jews, maybe even all female Jews, and I will make that my community. I'm going to preach to the converted and I'm going to be in a community where everyone agrees with me." It is very depressing and isolating to be so uncomfortable in the patriarchal community. But we have to fight the temptation to separate. We have to reach out . . . .

Norma:
But Elyse, we need a multilinear approach, not one. Not integrated all the time, not separated all the time. That is why I am so excited working with you, because we see the diversity and I think that's healthy. There is no one truth, no one way. We have to set a very wide agenda.

When you spoke about the newspaper article on Simchat Torah, Elyse, it reminded me of the time when our *chazen* (cantor) got up and asked, "Will all Jews who haven't had an *aliyah* yet on this *Simchat Torah* stand up?" When I said, "What about me," they treated it as a joke. On the other hand, when I had to study to find out whether I could carry the Torah on Simchat Torah, when I discovered that I could hold the Torah, dance with it, and proclaim it as my own, I was incredibly uplifted. I became very excited. Instead of detracting, my feminism made me go deeper, to learn more, although at times it certainly elevated the anger. Studying has enriched my understanding of what it is to be a Jew. It enhanced my sense of community, my knowledge of Judaism, and my desire to be a fully responsible, obligated member of this community, and I want them to let me in.

Naomi:
And you inspire other women to inspire the next generation, to counteract the loud message to younger women that says that they

can't have a place at the Torah or a place making an intellectual advance either inside or outside of Judaism. We need to teach them that they can. I think what we have to do as feminists is create a better, stronger community for the daughters who are following.

Elyse:

That's right. And so much of our community's sexism is based not on fact, or text, or learning, but on ignorance. So many times I have walked into a room and someone will say, "Oh, am I allowed to do that? Can I participate? I thought I couldn't." When asked where they got the idea that they couldn't, they would answer, "My mother told me, my rabbi mentioned it one day." If we could, as women, sit down and study the laws together we would learn to empower ourselves. And the next time someone says to us we are not allowed to do something we will say, "Yeah? You show me where in the text it says that! Sit down and study with me and prove where in the text it says I can't. If it says I can, I'm going to do it."

Norma:

We can study and pass what we learn on to women but there will be many who will still not hear us. We have to have patience for a longer vision down the road. When I first put on my *tallit*, the ritual prayer shawl that traditionally only men have worn, I had to examine why I wanted to, what it meant to me, linking me with my father and grandfather. I liked the essence of prayer and the wrapping up of oneself in individual meditation, of praying in community, but I also had to study to find out whether I could. So I studied all the laws and found out nothing prevented me. I could quote the *Gemarrah*, the *Shulchan Aruch* (the Jewish Code of Law), the *Rabbenu Tam*, from all the sources in our tradition by heart. So I wore the *tallit*. No matter what I said and no matter how many times my husband, who was the rabbi, wrote articles or gave sermons that affirmed my right to wear a *tallit*, everybody in the community was convinced one really could not, that I was entering the male world and it was a transgression to do that. So with all the lectures, with all the points of law, and with all the studying together, I am still an outsider. Maybe there will come a point in time, maybe the mass will reach a critical mass where enough women will be doing these things and studying these things that it will change.

Elyse:
For me it's an issue of privilege. People see a woman rabbi, a rabbi's wife, a learned woman and say, "She can do it. I can't but she can. Therefore we are isolated even more because it's that crazy woman or that rabbi over there. She gets the privilege. She's a different woman than the rest of us."

Norma:
I agree. It's a way of excluding us from community and as well, dealing with the threat that they think we may pose. If we say we can study, it doesn't mean or imply that they should be learning and studying more. I worry about being a role model but I also feel the pain of being excluded as that crazy woman. More than privilege, it is more a mechanism to claim women are not normative Jews. It is a mechanism for taking us off stage and making us marginal, not allowing our voices to be heard in a community of Judaism we'd like to make happen.

Naomi:
Men have set up so many divisions among women. So much of a woman's identity is tied up with men: you are identified with your

husband or you are identified with studying male texts, and these things give you status. The status of Jewish women depends so much on relationships with men. This sets up barriers among us. There are gay Jewish women who are not welcomed; they don't dare reveal themselves within the Jewish community. There are gay women rabbis who don't come out because they know they won't be accepted. My hope for feminist community is that it will break down these barriers among women.

Norma:
Cynthia Ozick once wrote "the only place I'm not a Jew is in my *shul*" and that has been one of the problems we have been discussing. The other side to this problem is that the only place I am not a feminist is usually in feminist circles, partly because I am a Jew and mainly because I am a religious Jew. I am a religious Jew trying to use the feminist critique to transform my community but I am still within that community and so really I am in no community. I am neither accepted completely within the synagogue world nor am I accepted in the feminist world.

Naomi:
I hope that's only temporary. I hope that things will change grad⁄ ually as we do work together and listen to one another. But right now I don't see much happening toward building Jewish feminist communities. Not yet. I think we have to do more talking. We have to do more writing. We have to do more speaking. I hunger for these things to happen.

Elyse:
Part of the reason it feels like so little is going on is because it is such an overwhelming task. Someone once said that being in a revolu⁄

tionary movement is like pushing an iceberg. You can't feel it moving but twenty years from now you step away and you say, "Oh my God, look how far that iceberg has moved." And I think Jewish feminists altogether, male and female, are pushing this iceberg. We are now taking Jewish rituals seriously: baby naming for girls, weaning ceremonies for mothers, even menstruation ceremonies for girls.

Naomi:
Study groups too.

Elyse:
Yes, study groups.

I am very involved in reclaiming the *mikvah* as a positive, beautiful, and holy symbol for women. I believe that we have to reclaim it because it has been ingrained in our psyche as being a dirty and ugly place. We need to use the *mikvah* as a constant reaffirmation of our purity as women, as Jews, and as people, not just a monthly connection to our menstrual cycles. We need to use the *mikvah* on Rosh Chodesh and on holidays when you want something to happen or when you are thankful that something has happened. Some people are uncomfortable with this concept.

Norma:
If you are trying to claim rituals, especially life-cycle rituals such as bat mitzvahs for girls, marriage ceremonies, birthing ceremonies, and *mikvah,* I also want to claim the world of textual study that has been reserved for men. I want to claim the right to study, also. I am trying to reach a point in my life where I establish my legitimacy as an interpreter of Jewish law. I can then set the stage for other women to participate in the process. I hope I am planting seeds amongst my

142

students as well as amongst my family of what possibilities there are for women. Yes, it is very slow but we are moving the iceberg. After the move, it will still be an iceberg. Naomi's question was where are we moving it to? I believe in my deepest sense is that what I am doing is an enrichment process, an invigoration, a liberation, and a growth for Judaism. It means that there will be more learned Jews and more Jews praying who are obligated to the responsibilities of Judaism. But we come close to borders and fine lines that evoke all kinds of fears.

Elyse:
In the moving of the iceberg, parts of it fall away and melt and some get chipped away and the question is, will the iceberg become smaller? What parts are we going to chip away . . . .

Norma:
I see the iceberg accumulating as we move it, and it will still be Judaism and the Jewish community, growing and dynamic as it has always been. I want that dynamism and that growth to allow room for me, for my children, and for a community in which women too are considered the norm, central, and Jews.

Naomi:
How about diversity? Do you see a place for diverse interpretations of what it means to be a Jew within that community or do you see these interpretations creating different communities, like little islands of ice floating separately in the sea? I would hope that communities with varied interpretations of Judaism could talk to one another. I would want to see tolerance and respect. Unfortunately, I don't see a lot of these qualities in the Jewish community right now.

143

Norma:

I don't see it now. I hope we will get there. I do believe in diversity and plurality — the iceberg has many peaks and little islands. It is all an accumulation but it is not monolithic or uniform by any means. I would hope that we grow together in communities, with respect for each other and for each other's ways of finding the way called Judaism.

Elyse:

Women are doing it. When you look at the Jewish feminist move-ment you see orthodox, conservative, reform, secular, reconstruc-tion, zionist, and interfaith women together. When we get together as Jewish women we are teaching men that Jews can talk to each other. That is a very feminist model.

Norma:

When the women in the Conservative movement wanted the sem-inary to allow women to study for the rabbinate, they were joined by Orthodox, Reform and secular Jewish feminists who fought alongside for it. Whether it was going to happen to me or not was not the issue. It was important to expand the vision, to be inclusive of women. I want to live in a world where we sing many tunes; we sometimes harmonize but we learn from each other and grow together.

⸿ Shulamit Aloni is a lawyer in Jerusalem and as leader of the Citizen's Rights Party, is a member of the Israeli Knesset where she is one of the very few women. She has been a key participant in searching for civil legal answers for Jewish legal problems in Israel. Since the completion of the film, Half the Kingdom, *Shulamit Aloni has been appointed Minister of Education in the Labour government.*

SHULAMIT ALONI

Women in Israeli politics

The established Jewish women's organizations are not struggling for women's rights. They are struggling for the wife and the mother, and usually they are organized to support men and the establishment. They cannot stand women fighting against the establishment, and that is why they did not like the feminists groups that started in Israel. And they don't like a woman who fights for what she believes in and who is in the Opposition. They love me to talk against the religious establishment but they cannot tolerate me talking of political life — against the Government, against the Prime Minister. If I was a man I think they would not mind so much. If I was part of the establishment, talking about peace in this part of the world and our relations with the P.L.O., et cetera, it would be accepted. But to be a woman in the Opposition in the Knesset they cannot stand it.

Jewish women are brought up to support the establishment, to support the power of men, as a wife, an organization, a group, but they do not ask men and other organizations to support them in the fight for equal rights. Jewish women are the supporters and they want some fringe benefits for themselves. There are only small groups of Jewish women in Israel who are able to make changes and are ready to do it. Feminist groups have great difficulty in achieving major breakthroughs on women's issues. The only leaders that have emerged over the last twenty or thirty years from the large mainstream organizations like Pioneer Women (Na'amat) and Hadassah (WIZO), despite their leadership seminars, are support-ers of the large parties and 'big' power. So we have a long way to go but I think we will do it.

There is a myth that Israeli women have equal rights and equal opportunities because Golda Meir was Prime Minister. India had Indira Gandhi as Prime Minister as well, and the question is how much closer did the women of India get to achieving equal rights and opportunities? Did either of them improve the status of women? In Israel women are drafted into the army and they do the usual jobs that women do in the army, including serving coffee. Put in coffee machines and allow the generals to serve themselves.

The status of women in Israel is a kind of paradox. On one hand we have two women judges in the Supreme Court and I think that is great because this is the highest rank a person can achieve. On the other hand, those two women cannot sit on a bench in a family court, which is the lowest court in the land. Not only can they not sit on the bench just because they are women, they cannot be proper witnesses in court, and any documents they sign as witnesses are nullified because they are women. So here you have the Israeli problem of the status of women. In Israel they worship the wife and the mother, but the woman as a human being in control of her own destiny, that is something completely different.

In marriage and divorce the wife is still her husband's property. Only he can divorce her. He can have as many women as he wants and have children from every one of them; the children will be considered legitimate children if the women are single. If a wife is deserted by her husband for many years and she tries to rebuild her life with somebody else, she will be considered as a whore and an adulteress and her children will be *mamzerim*, bastards. These children will be excommunicated for ten generations and won't be able to marry in Israel and in religious ceremonies elsewhere.

Some say there cannot be change. I believe that change is possible but as long as we are under the jurisdiction of the clergy from cradle to grave, there is not much hope. It is the same for Jews under the Jewish clergy, Moslems under the Moslem clergy, and Christians under the Christian clergy. It is a legacy from the seventh century when the Arabs conquered this part of the world. Unfortunately Israel has a backward, fanatical, and ignorant religious establish-ment and they want to impose on us laws which might have been up-to-date three thousand years ago. Society has changed since then.

In every place in the world where a religious establishment has money and power, political power, you will find that women's rights — human rights — are ignored and abused. This is the case in Israel. The clergy use primeval fears and superstitious attitudes to manoeuvre the people. Today you have a worshipping of power, and nationalism together with the religious establishment. When Mussolini was young he was anti-religious and a socialist. When he came to power and wanted to rebuild the old Roman Empire, he had a pact with the Pope. In Spain, Franco had the cooperation of the Church; the same thing occurred in Hungary, in Greece, and in many other places. Now we are facing the same situation in Israel. The religious establishment is becoming stronger because of its ideological stance that the Jews are the Chosen People. This is the Promised Land. The Arabs are like the seven Canaanic tribes.

By-passing the religious establishment

It is difficult to have a breakthrough but it is possible. One way of creating a breakthrough is to by-pass the religious establishment. Instead of following the marriage and divorce laws which are controlled by the clergy, use marriage contracts which come under the law of contracts. Under the law of contracts marriage and children are legitimate. Hundreds of couples are avoiding the religious courts. The religious authorities can also be side-stepped by using the Declaration of Independence, which speaks for equality, and using the Supreme Court against the religious and political establishment, for instance using the Declaration to allow women to sit on the decision-making body which votes on and then elects rabbis.

I received an emergency call from a family in crisis. A young couple from a prominent *sephardic* family made preparations for their marriage. They invited more than a thousand people to the wedding. The bride-to-be was a twenty-one year-old *olah*, or new immigrant, from South Africa. Her mother converted to Judaism thirty years ago in South Africa and is married to a man who is very Orthodox. Nevertheless, at the last moment, the Israeli rabbinate refused to marry the couple because they did not accept the mother's conversion thirty years ago. Now a thousand guests had already been invited. The couple felt completely lost and they called me. I made-up the ceremony for them, with a contract. It began with a nice preamble which included statements on equality and love and the show went on. This is one example of people who were in a terrible situation created by the clergy. The public knows about this case because it was reported on television. And now I see more and more cases like this where the couple is under pressure and cannot marry.

There are many others who do not want to go to the rabbinical courts because they believe in the equality of men and women and do not want a religious ceremony.

I know of a case where a woman acquired a *get*, a divorce decree, in a Conservative rabbinical court in San Francisco, and remarried. The rabbis in Israel did not recognize the divorce and therefore considered that she was still married to her previous husband. When her daughter came to Israel, the rabbis decided that she was not Jewish and was a bastard because her mother was, basically, a whore.

The clergy attempts to rule Jews all over the world through the 'Who is a Jew?' debate. They have black lists gleaned from rabbis around the world who support their position. There is something anti-Jewish about this because Judaism never had a pope. According to Jewish tradition every community appoints its rabbi. Perhaps because the clergy in Israel came from Eastern Europe which was dominated by the Catholic church, they want the same kind of power. Or perhaps they have the appetite to make Israel a Khomani-style country. If you refer to Israel's (changing) Law of Return, the rabbis want to supervise the laws pertaining to immigration, citizenship, and registration. They want to eliminate all ideas of pluralism in Judaism.

I do not agree with the premise that if you have more women in power, more women in Parliament, they will do better than men as far as peace is concerned. When Golda Meir was Prime Minister there was the terrible Yom Kippur War. There was a war when Margaret Thatcher, Prime Minister of Britain was in power. And Indira Gandhi had various conflicts. My colleague in the Knesset, Geula Cohen, is prepared to deport or kill each and every Arab.

Israel is fighting for its survival and people like myself, who don't have another place to go to and don't want to go anywhere else, must look for ways to bring about peace. This includes talking with Ashav, the Opposition. On this issue and on every issue men and women must work together.

Adelman, Penina. *Miriam's Well*. Fresh Meadows, New York: Biblio Press, 1986.

Antler, Joyce. *America and I: Short Stories by American Jewish Women Writers*. Boston: Beacon Press, 1990.

Baum, Charlotte, Paula Hyman, and Sonya Michel. *The Jewish Woman in America*. New York: Dial, 1976.

Beck, Evelyn Torton. *Nice Jewish Girls: A Lesbian Anthology*. Watertown, Mass.: Persephone Press, 1982.

Berkovits, Eliezer. *Jewish Women in Time and Torah*. New York: Ktav, 1990.

Biale, Rachel. *Women and Jewish Law*. New York: Schocken, 1984.

Bletter, Diana and Grinker, Lori. *The Invisible Thread*. Philadelphia: Jewish Publication Society, 1989.

Broner, E.M. *Her Mothers*. New York: Holt, Rinehart & Winston, 1978.

_____ . *A Weave of Women* New York: Holt, Rinehart & Winston, 1978.

_____ , and Cathy N. Davidson, eds. *The Lost Tradition: Mothers and Daughters in Literature*. New York: Ungar, 1980.

Cantor, Aviva. *The Jewish Woman: 1900–1980. An Annotated Bibliography*. New York: Biblio Press, 1981.

Cohen, Arthur and Mendes-Flohr, Paul. *Contemporary Jewish Religious Thought*. New York: Scribners, 1987.

Donin, Haim. *To Be a Jew*. New York: Basic Books, 1972.

Feldman, David. *Birth Control in Jewish Law: Marital Relations, Contraception, and Abortion*. New York: New York University Press, 1968.

Frankiel, Tamar. *The Voice of Sarah — Feminine Spirituality and Traditional Judaism*. Harper, San Francisco, 1990.

Freedman, Marcia. *Exile in the Promised Land*. Ithaca, New York: Firebrand Books, 1990.

Goldenberg, Naomi R. *The Changing of the Gods: Feminism and the End of Traditional Religions*. Boston: Beacon Press, 1979.

_____ . *Returning Words to Flesh: Feminism, Psychoanalysis, and the Resurrection of the Body*. Boston: Beacon Press, 1990.

Greenberg, Blu. *On Women and Judaism: A View from Tradition*. Philadelphia: Jewish Publication Society, 1981.

Henry, Sondra and Emily Taitz. *Written Out of History*. Fresh Meadows, New York: Biblio Press, 1983.

Heschel, Susannah, ed. *On Being a Jewish Feminist: A Reader*. New York: Schocken, 1983.

Kaye Krantrowitz, Melanie. *My Jewish Face and Other Stories*. San Francisco: Spinsters/Aunt Lute Book Company, 1990.

Klepfisz, Irena. *A Few Words in the Mother Tongue: Poems Selected and New (1971–90)*. Portland: The Eighth Mountain Press, 1991.

_____ . *Dreams of an Insomniac: Jewish Feminist Essays, Speeches and Diatribes*. Portland: The Eighth Mountain Press, 1991.

Landsberg, Michele. *Women and Children First*. Markham, Ont.: Penguin, 1982.

Mazow, Julia Wolf. *The Woman Who Lost Her Names: Selected Writings of American Jewish Women*. San Francisco: Harper & Row, 1980.

Ochs, Vanessa. *Words on Fire: One Woman's Journey into the Sacred*. New York: Harcourt Brace, Jovanovich, 1990.

Plaskow, Judith. *Standing Again at Sinai: Judaism from a Feminist Perspective*. San Francisco: Harper & Row, 1989.

Schneider, Susan Weidman. *Jewish and Female: Choices and Changes in Our Lives Today*. Simon & Schuster, 1985.

_____ . *Intermarriage: The Challenge of Living with Differences Between Christians and Jews*. New York: The Free Press, 1989.

Sered, Susan Starr. *Women as Ritual Experts: The Religious Lives of Elderly Jewish Women in Jerusalem*. New York: Oxford University Press, 1992.

Taking the Fruit: A collection of women's rituals from the Women's Institute for Continuing Eduction, San Diego.

Umansky, Ellen and Dale Ashton, eds. *Four Centuries of Jewish Women's Spirituality: A Source Book*. Boston: Beacon Press, 1992.

Weiss, Avraham. *Women at Prayer*. New York: Ktav, 1990.

Francine Zuckerman has worked as a film director and producer for the past ten years. A graduate of McGill University, where she studied film, Zuckerman worked in radio, video and still photog-raphy before she directed *Half the Kingdom* — a National Film Board, Studio D co-production. She was the recipient of the Budge Crawley Fellowship at the Summer Institute of Film and Video, Ottawa, 1987. She is presently developing a new documentary entitled *Sacred Space* and has begun work on her first dramatic feature, *A Weave of Women*, based on E.M. Broner's novel.